D1456327

SUPER
BOOM

SUPER BOOM

WHY THE DOW WILL HIT 38,820 AND HOW YOU CAN PROFIT FROM IT

JEFFREY A. HIRSCH

WILEY

John Wiley & Sons, Inc.

Published by John Wiley & Sons, Inc., Hoboken, New Jersey.
Published simultaneously in Canada.

For general information on our other products and services or for technical support, please contact our Customer Care Department within the United States at (800) 762-2974, outside the United States at (317) 572-3993 or fax (317) 572-4002.

Wiley also publishes its books in a variety of electronic formats. Some content that appears in print may not be available in electronic books. For more information about Wiley products, visit our web site at www.wiley.com.

ISBN 978-1-118-02470-6 (cloth); ISBN 978-1-118-07533-3 (ebk);
ISBN 978-1-118-07534-0 (ebk); ISBN 978-1-118-07535-7 (ebk)

Printed in the United States of America

10 9 8 7 6 5 4 3 2 1

This book is humbly dedicated to Yale Hirsch, my illustrious father and mentor—man of many talents, great thoughts, and big ideas. An iconoclastic market thinker, who made the greatest market call in history in 1976 for a 500 percent move in the market from the 1974 low to 1990. Thank you for giving me the business and all your love and support these past 44 years. Not only did you teach me the market, but you taught me how to appreciate all things in life. I proudly stand on your shoulders and prudently ride the coattails of your life's work.

To my knowledge, Yale was the first to call the bottom of the last secular bear market in October 1974 and the first to predict the last super boom in March 1976.

Contents

PART III

Booms and Busts of the Twentieth Century

PART IV

The Prodigal Pattern Returns

Foreword

Nearly every trading desk on Wall Street has a copy of the *Stock Trader's Almanac* on it. That's not an exaggeration—if you travel to the offices of enough Wall Street banks, mutual funds, and hedge funds, you'll see plenty of dog-eared copies of the *Almanac*.

That is how I first met Jeff Hirsch—reading the *STA*. I began my career in finance working as a trader. In my first job on a trading desk, we newbies received very little training. We were thrown into the deep end of the pool, and if you managed to avoid drowning—poof!—you were a trader. It was all very Darwinian.

Those of us who managed to survive learned quickly of the many things that affected how markets traded. Valuation, liquidity, sentiment, technical, and interest rate trends all moved stocks and bonds. But there was something larger at work that we did not see in the day-to-day trading. If you stepped back far enough to observe longer arcs of time, you could see a certain cycle. Indeed, it became apparent that markets moved with a certain rhythm, with variations of specific patterns repeating over and over again.

The *Stock Trader's Almanac* was the first source I encountered that quantified these cycles. Whether it was the pattern of triple witch option expirations, or the seasonal best six months of the year, the *STA* provided a framework to view market history through the lens of repeating cycles.

History repeating ("Rhyming," according to a quote attributed to Mark Twain) was the spark that sent me hunting for a broader view of how markets work. Why do stocks rise and fall? What factors drive short- and long-term prices? Why do valuations fluctuate so much?

Jeff and Yale Hirsch are the father–son duo behind the *Almanac*. They each spent much of their careers as the editor/ publisher of the book—Yale from 1966–2000 and Jeff from 2000 to the present day. But they also have something else in common: They are students of market history. This has led them to rather nonmainstream understandings of the work- ings of the stock market. Seasonal data, longer-term trends, and historical cycles are part of their repertoire.

Besides the genetics, they have something else in common: Their understanding of secular markets and historical patterns has led each of them to make an outrageous forecast from the depths of a market collapse. The same historical, cyclical, and mathematical analyses underlay each of their predictions, made three and a half decades apart. Postwar peace dividends, excess inflation from war and crisis spending, and rapid adop- tion of new technologies are the factors that drove the prior secular market booms, and according to Jeff, will drive the next one as well.

Let's look at a bit of history: In the spring of 1976, in the middle of a terrible decade that saw very little progress in equi- ties, rampant inflation, an oil embargo, several recessions, the end of a very unpopular war, and a presidential resignation, Yale Hirsch made a very unusual forecast. From those dark days of disco and polyester, he predicted a 500 percent move in the markets. Even more surprising, he hit the bull's-eye.

When you consider the context, it is an unlikely, even absurd forecast. The Dow had kissed 1,000 back in 1966. In 1974, it was still 40 percent below that level. Inflation was ram- pant, recessions seemed to come along every few years, and the country was still reeling from the double blows of Vietnam and Watergate. Ten years into what would turn out to be a 16-year period of zero market progress (1966–1982), the Dow was flat in nominal terms. Adjusted for inflation, it was down almost 45 percent.

How could Yale make such a forecast? The historian in him noticed something interesting about markets. It seemed that inflation surged during each of the world wars. That was followed by a 500 percent catch-up rally in equities after each war ended. With the end of the Vietnam War, could markets three-peat?

Indeed, that was the basis of Yale's prediction: In a special report in *Smart Money,* he estimated that from the 1974 intra-day low of Dow 570, the Dow would rise 500 percent by 1990, hitting 3,420. The S&P did gain 500 percent from its 1974 low to high in July 1990. The Dow crossed 3,420 in May 1992—off by a few years, but all things considered, a terrific and money-making call.

Thirty-five years later, Yale's son Jeff has made a similar forecast. According to the author of this book, the next super boom cycle will follow a decade of wars in Iraq and Afghanistan. It will send the Dow Jones to 38,820 by 2025.

I certainly don't need to explain how outrageous this forecast is—but I want to distinguish it from the 1990s dot-com excesses. We saw ridiculous books with titles like *Dow 36,000* and even *Dow 100,000.* These were indicia of bubble mania. Sentiment had run wild; the belief that valuations no longer mattered was becoming increasingly accepted. Out of this mania came some pretty awful—and for investors, money-losing—tomes. They were based on theories subsequently shown to be false, leavened with excess optimism, the recency effect, and a lack of critical analysis.

Numerous factors distinguish this book and its outrageous forecast from those that preceded it:

This book was written in the depths of a bear market collapse and recession—not in the final spasms of an 18-year bull market.

It is based on historical patterns that have held true three times during the twentieth century following each of its major wars.

It is contrary to the conventional wisdom, rather than an excessive extension of it.

When Jeff first announced this forecast, it caused a stir. Several media pundits dismissed it out of hand; they had already been burned by *Dow 36,000*, and they were not going to make that mistake twice.

However, of all these books that made seemingly ridiculous market forecasts, I would not be too quick to dismiss this one. It is based on a sound methodology, from a student of market history. It forecasts that the secular bear market that began in March 2000 continues for a few more years, than gives way to technological innovation and ensuing prosperity. But it's not all roses, as Jeff also identifies the risk of our crisis-managed economy. Inflation, which accompanied the prior three periods of postwar prosperity, is a major risk factor over the next two decades.

It is thought-provoking stuff. I hope you find it as fascinating as I have.

—BARRY RITHOLTZ
January 2011

Acknowledgments

Writing a book is an adventure. To begin with it is a toy, an amusement; then it is a mistress, and then a master, and then a tyrant.

—Winston Churchill

In addition to the groundbreaking work Yale Hirsch has done over the past four decades, especially in the mid-1970s, this book draws heavily on the work of Judd Taylor Brown while he was vice president and director of research at the Hirsch Organization from 2000 to 2009. Judd and I resurrected Yale's 1974 "BUY!" recommendation in 2002 and developed the three-part series in our *Almanac Investor Newsletter* on how war and peace impacts the market in late 2004 and early 2005. We collaborated on the first manifestation of the current 500 percent super boom move forecast on page 42 of *Stock Trader's Almanac 2006*. The research, analysis, and writing Judd produced while employed at the Hirsch Organization was relied upon profoundly in this book. I wish him all the best in his new culinary pursuits.

This book would not have been possible without the herculean efforts of Christopher Mistal, who tirelessly brainstormed with me, researched, edited, cajoled, and supported me in this project in every way conceivable. It is his calm demeanor, critical thinking, and software development that is the glue of the Hirsch Organization.

I'd like to thank the editorial team at Wiley for their enthusiasm about turning this forecast into a book: Pamela van Giessen, Kevin Commins, Peter Knapp, Cristin Riffle-Lash, and most of all, my new editor, Evan Burton, who diligently guided this project to completion in an incredibly short period of time.

I'd also like to thank Barry Ritholtz for agreeing to write the Foreword and always being a candid voice of reason and inspiration to me personally and to the world through his ever-salient financial blog, The Big Picture.

And last but certainly not least, my wife, Jennifer, and our two boys, Sam and Nate, my muses. Thanks for understanding my tight deadline and letting Daddy write on countless nights and weekends. I owe you big time.

—JEFFREY A. HIRSCH

SUPER
BOOM

ANATOMY OF A SUPER BOOM

Dow 38,820 by 2025 may seem incredible at this current juncture in our economic, political, and financial history, but as you will find out throughout these pages, it is mathematically reasonable and requires no big leap of faith. Moves of this magnitude have happened several times before at similar points in history with such regularity and clear causes that you will agree by the book's end that the potential for another super boom is undeniable.

When *Stock Trader's Almanac 2011* first hit the street in October 2010 and this forecast became widely known, skeptics wrote, e-mailed, blogged, and invited me on the air for cross-examination. My good friend and colleague Barry Ritholtz e-mailed me the same three letters he posted to his blog, *The Big Picture*: "WTF?" After explaining the logic behind my prediction, he followed that up with a post that the move was well within the average annual historic market gains. Despite the initial skepticism, others began to agree a boom was possible.

But why make such a bold forecast? Many before me have been burned by predictions that never came to be. It amazes me how well remembered the follies are and how forgotten the bulls'-eyes.

The simple answer is because I believe it will happen. My father's super boom prediction in 1976 was historic. Since inheriting the family business I've kept a careful lookout for signs of another super boom. Several years ago, those signs began to emerge.

From December 2004 to February 2005, we at the Hirsch Organization ran a three-part piece on war and peace and the market in our *Almanac Investor eNewsletter*. The full piece first appeared on page 42 of the *Stock Trader's Almanac 2006*. Our 2006 book, *The Almanac Investor: Profit from Market History and Seasonal Trends* (Wiley 2006) also featured a chapter on "How War and Peace Impact the Markets," including the prospects for a 500 percent move.

Part One answers the foundational questions about 500 percent market moves, or what I've dubbed super booms: What are they? Where do they come from? What causes them and what is their impact on the market? This part also addresses the current economy and its role in the next super boom.

CHAPTER 1

The Boom Equation

*We always live in an uncertain world. What is certain is that
the United States will go forward over time.*

—Warren Buffett

When we made our super boom prediction in fall
2010 that the Dow would reach 38,820 by 2025, many people
reacted with stunned disbelief. With unemployment high, the
great recession hardly in the rearview mirror, mounting global debt, and most people saturated with negative news from
friends and family, skepticism was rampant. That came as no
surprise to us—all bold predictions are first lambasted before
proven true.

Throughout this book, we demonstrate that the coming
super boom is not only plausible, but mathematically and historically probable. Moves of this magnitude have happened
several times throughout history, and they have always been
preceded by tumultuous times and economic weakness. In
fact, big moves happen with such regularity and clear cause
that we have successfully identified why they happen, how they
happen, and when they happen. Most importantly, we show

3

what to invest in before and as they happen. By examining the past, we are able to shed light on the future.

The Late, Great Technician

Few stock market prognosticators could call 'em as well as the late, great technician, George Lindsay. An intense student of market cycles and repetitive price patterns, George could, from memory, reproduce a chart of stock market prices for every one of the last 150 years. We started publishing George's work in 1968 in our first *Stock Trader's Almanac*. At the time, George was editor of *George Lindsay's Opinion*, a highly respected newsletter that predicted the course of the stock market for the calendar year month by month. We featured his forecast for 1968 in our first *Almanac* and it was a breathtaking bull's-eye. In the following year, we presented his groundbreaking pattern for identifying market tops in price charts using technical analysis, what he called Three Peaks and the Domed House. It was 63 years ago that George discovered the Three Peaks pattern he would become famous for.

George made numerous predictions, both bold and accurate. In 1987, John Brown, who had merged the Lindsay letter into his own, *The Advisor*, published a letter directly from George dated July 1, 1987. George died shortly thereafter, but not before communicating his prescient feeling to Brown that, "It now seems likely that the last high will come some time in August 1987." Again, he was right on the money. Beginning on August 25, 1987, from a high of 2,722.42, the Dow fell 40.6 percent over 39 trading days to an intraday low of 1,616.21 on October 20, 1987.

In 1991, four years after George's death, in recognition of the outstanding contributions he made to the field of technical analysis, the Market Technicians Association bestowed its Annual Award upon George Lindsay.

George's most impressive forecast was made in July 1969 (see Figure 1.1). Appearing in our *1970 Stock Trader's Almanac*,

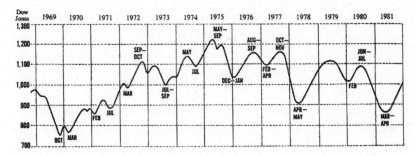

FIGURE 1.1 George Lindsay's Prediction

it showed the Dow gaining virtually no ground over the next 12 years. As the years unfolded, the Dow spent most of its time in the 800–1,000 range, in line with George's forecast. George's prediction as it appeared on page 41 of the *1970 Stock Trader's Almanac* is compared to the Dow's actual performance from 1969 to 1981 (Figure 1.2).

Of course, George had no way of foretelling what disasters and problematic events would occur during the dozen years covered in his forecast. The Cambodian invasion in 1970; the

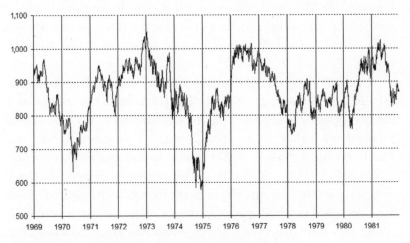

FIGURE 1.2 Dow Jones Industrials, 1969–1981

oil embargo by the OPEC cartel in late 1973 and the subsequent quintupling of oil prices; and the taking of American hostages in Iran in 1979 may have knocked the market a little off course from George's forecast. But he was unmistakably, remarkably close.

Inspired by George's prediction, my father, Yale Hirsch, began looking at the 500 percent stock market boom after World War I in the 1920s (a speculative bubble fueled by low margins), as well as the 12 tough years that followed, containing the twentieth century's only depression and a stagnant stock market. After the World War II victory rally, the market drifted, going virtually nowhere from May 1946 to June 1949. But from the bottom in June 1949, the Dow logged another 500 percent bull cycle during the 1950s and 1960s to the top in February 1966.

As George had anticipated, the previous boom and bust pattern repeated itself with a similar 12 years of consolidation from 1969 through 1981. In other words, the cycle of war and peace followed by runaway inflation and inflation followed by a 500 percent move in the stock market had developed into a predictable pattern. With that as the background, Yale predicted in March 1976 that the Dow would rise to 3,420 by 1990, based on this simple equation: war + peacetime + inflation = 500 percent rise. Yale's prediction of Dow 3,420 was a 500 percent move from the 1974 intraday low of 570.

I was 10 years old when Yale made this incredible forecast. Weaned on recurring stock market patterns, I remember as a child flippantly assessing stock chart patterns in my pajamas as I kissed my father goodnight. Though I fought entering the family business with youthful pride, as this prediction turned into reality, I was drawn into the business. When the S&P 500 hit the 500 percent move mark in July 1990 and the Dow crossed 3,420 in 1992, I was hooked and set out on a course to build and improve upon Yale's groundbreaking forecast and lifelong work.

Finding the Next Five Hundred

The first inklings of another potential 500 percent move in the stock market began to materialize in September 2002 as the first major downdraft of the secular bear market that began in January 2000 with the dot-com crash came to a close. The war drums were beating to invade Iraq, and the stock market was plunging going into the midterm elections. After four bullish e-mail alerts in early October as the market capitulated, on October 16, 2002, seven days after what would later be recognized as the market bottom, I published the headline "BUY! BUY! BUY!" 18 times across the top of the *Almanac Investor eNewsletter*.

This contrary point of view and gutsy prognostication brought an onslaught of e-mail and telephone calls from irate readers shocked at how I could make such an irresponsible recommendation at such a dire time for the country, the market, and the world. Contrarian investing is *believing* you are right when market sentiment, pundits, and even subscribers tell you you're wrong. Though it made me uneasy, I trusted in my methodology and was convinced that since so few agreed, I must be on the right track.

This bold buy prediction hearkened back to my father, Yale Hirsch's, October 1974 "BUY! BUY! BUY!" headline and set in motion a process over the next eight years that culminates now in the super boom forecast.

I latched on to the potential for a long, sideways period similar to what George Lindsay forecasted in 1970 in our *Almanac Investor eNewsletter* 2003 Annual Forecast. Our initial forecast of a Dow in the 7,000–11,000 range was tempered by the awareness that exogenous events could expand or augment that range. As we saw from 2007 to 2009, the credit bubble pushed up the top end of that range, and the financial crisis deepened the low end.

Our long-term outlook for the market was restrained, and we expected it to behave as it did in the 1970s, going sideways for 12 years. We said, *"We would not be surprised for the Dow to remain range-bound between 7,000 and 11,000 for the better part of the decade unless of course the global hot spots implode, oil prices go through the roof, and economies worldwide fall apart.*" For the past several years we have traded the patterns, remained alert to exogenous events, and responded to changing conditions and important market indicators.

How War and Peace (and Inflation) Impact the Market

In December 2004, we began a monthly three-part series analyzing the impact of war and peace and inflation on the markets. The intent was to discover and document the anatomy as well as the nuances of a historical cycle based on Yale's original work in 1976 (and on George Lindsay's original work in 1969), studying the patterns that caused super booms. If we could isolate, identify, and extrapolate the indicators and patterns, we believed we could use those data to spot the next big stock market and economic boom.

The first question we needed to answer was what makes the market range bound during wartime and rise during peacetime? The simple answer is inflation. The government empties the treasury during a war. It also focuses on foreign issues rather than domestic concerns and the economy. The result is a sustained rise in inflation. Only after the economy settles down and Washington refocuses on domestic issues will the stock market soar to new heights.

History never repeats itself exactly, but an understanding of stock market behavior during the three major wars of the twentieth century provided important insight into market action during the current war in Iraq and Afghanistan and on terror. Here are the keys.

Four Basic Tenets of Wartime Markets

1. *No significant new highs.* The Dow has never made a significant high during wartime. The lack of a big breakout can

be attributed to muted investor enthusiasm. Every time the market tried to break out of its range, inevitably a negative exogenous event pertaining to the war, another crisis, or economic weakness of some kind dampened spirits. The market fleetingly poked above the previous highs as it did in 1973 and 2007, but the moves were short-lived and not technically significant.

2. *The war machine props up the market.* After the initial shock of a new war, the market forms a floor near the prewar low. The combination of government spending, investor bargain hunting, and good old American pride help insulate the market from breaching that prewar low.

3. *The market (as always) is a barometer.* Markets rally on sustained good news and fall on sustained bad news. The markets also tend to be more reactive early in wartime. By the end of a prolonged engagement, investors tend to be more callous about news. The markets will also anticipate the end of the war by moving to a high-water mark. This contributes to the inevitable letdown when peace breaks out.

4. *Wartime presidents do not lose.* Presidents tend to shape their political decisions pertaining to a foreign war around the presidential election cycle, making unpopular decisions only after they are reelected, while creating as much good news as possible leading up to the election. The rhetoric from the incumbent administration is always that conditions are improving, while challengers call for change. Domestic issues, a weak ticket from the incumbent party, low approval ratings for the president, and the lack of a sitting president or strong VP running ushered a new party into the White House in 2008. Like Harding in 1920 and Nixon in 1968, Obama came into office with a country clamoring for change.

Not Your Daddy's CPI

Inflation increases significantly during wartime as Figure 1.3 illustrates. Very simply, war is expensive. The upsurge in inflation brought on by war is the catalyst for huge gains in the markets once peace and prosperity return. During the three previous 500 percent stock market moves—or for that matter, the last hundred years—war and subsequent inflation have been constants.

There are challenges in evaluating the inflationary pattern this time around. The U.S. Department of Labor's Bureau of Labor Statistics (BLS) has tweaked and manipulated the Consumer Price Index (CPI) so many times over the past 30 years or so in an attempt to mask inflation that the indicator may very well not detect a true upsurge in inflation in the years ahead. No one is really sure how this new and improved version of the CPI will react in a hyperinflationary environment. We may see a 40 percent to 50 percent increase in the CPI—or we may see another 200 percent rise.

We consider the CPI a dubious metric at best. The BLS has become obsessed in its efforts to tweak the data. Modern calculations, we feel, do not represent real-world inflation rates. Small increases in the government's assessment of inflation are significantly larger in the real world. But regardless of our grousing, it remains the prime standard in gauging inflation for economists and investors.

Going forward, the value of the dollar, the increased cost of a gallon of milk, or a can of chicken noodle soup, may be a better measurement of inflation than the CPI. The important idea is that prices are going to rise sharply in the near future, which will power the next secular bull market as it has in past postwar economies.

During these postwar booms, the Dow moved up despite many unsettling events: the Korean War; the French defeat and withdrawal from Vietnam; McCarthyism; revolts in Poland, Hungary, Argentina; the Egyptian seizure of the Suez Canal and war with Israel, France, and Britain; the civil rights movement; the Cuban missile crisis; the Kennedy assassination; and more. No market follows historical trends perfectly; however, the biggest trends, the most important, all have an impact. The first step is identifying which events will have impact. The second is measuring and forecasting the size of that impact.

War: What Is It Good For?

Without doubt, the single most important noncyclical influence impacting the stock market is war. That nine years of foreign conflict may be drawing to an end bodes well for the markets. As the chart in Figure 1.3 illustrates, the market has failed to make any significant headway so long as the country is embroiled in a significant and lasting conflict.

The markets have been stuck in a trading range since the dot-com stock market bubble popped in 2000 and the Iraq War began on March 19, 2003. While there have been large rallies and pullbacks, there has been no real advance since 2000. Moves that leave the previous highs behind for good— the greater than 500 percent moves that have historically occurred between all of the major wars the United States has been involved in—have not happened.

Figure 1.3, "500+ Percent Moves Follow Inflation," provides the big picture. The Dow and the CPI are plotted together with highlighted sections showing the long-term range-bound markets surrounding World War I, World War II, and Vietnam. The long super booms and bull markets are bracketed with the Dow's performance. The correlation between war, inflation, and the subsequent catch-up of the market is impossible to ignore. Consolidation during wartime possesses roughly the same percentage range, giving the appearance of launching pads for the 500 percent moves. The inflation/catch-up correlation is clear. World War I inflation (up 110 percent) was followed by the 504 percent rise in the stock prices during the 1920s. The inflation of World War II (up 74 percent) led to a rise of the Dow of 523 percent. Finally, the inflation due to the Vietnam conflict of over 200 percent and the subsequent super bull market with the Dow rising 1,447 percent is a stunning corroboration of the historic pattern.

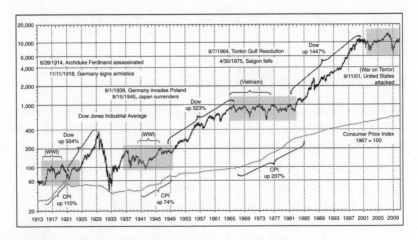

FIGURE 1.3 500+ Percent Moves Follow Inflation
Source: © Stock Trader's Almanac.
CPI source: Bureau of Labor Statistics.

Booms and Busts of the Twentieth Century

As government spending increased dramatically in response to the global financial crisis and the Great Recession, it is clear there is more at play than just wartime inflation coming home to roost. But it's important to realize that all three previous secular bear markets associated with the three major wars of the twentieth century were also affected by financial crises that required a great deal of non-war-related spending to stave off. The subsequent booms were driven by peace, inflation from war and crisis spending, and enabling technologies that created major cultural paradigm shifts and sustained prosperity.

The Rich Man's Panic of 1901–1903 and the panic of 1907 preceded World War I. Henry Ford perfected his automobile assembly line in 1913 as World War I was brewing, but cars did not really begin to replace horses until after the war, at which point the stock market boomed.

World War II helped get us out of the Great Depression. But it was not until the rise of the middle class in the 1950s, when our predominantly agrarian society morphed into a more industrialized and more urban society and demand surged for houses, appliances, and cars, that the stock market took off again. And the television connected the nation and the world.

As the Vietnam War began to wind down in the mid-1970s, oil crises, Watergate, and Mideast turmoil plunged America into stagflation, that nasty combination of recession and inflation. The advent of personal computers drove the first phase of the last super boom. Then, the Internet and cell phones created the Information Revolution, fueling the greatest boom since the Industrial Revolution.

Super booms of the past were conceived during wartime and financial crises, which produced elevated government spending, rising inflation, and pent-up demand. They were weaned on peace, stable political leadership, and effective governing. Finally, they were fed a steady diet of cultural paradigm shifting, enabling technology that changed the world and the way the average person lived. As the boom gains traction and heightened consumer spending spurs business and economic growth, the so-called "animal spirits" of businesses, entrepreneurs, and investors are restored, shifting the boom into high gear. Finally, the boom reaches overdrive before falling back to earth.

We are not there yet, but that is where we are headed.

CHAPTER 2

A Strangled Economy

Bear markets don't act like a medicine ball rolling down a smooth hill. Instead, they behave like a basketball bouncing down a rock-strewn mountainside; there's lots of movement up and sideways before the bottom is reached.
                    —Daniel Turov, *Barron's*, May 21, 2001

One other person called the 1974 bottom nearly as early as Yale Hirsch did, my good friend and colleague, Daniel Turov. Two months after Yale's "BUY!" recommendation in his *Smart Money* newsletter on October 1, 1974, Dan's "Buy Signal? A New Technical Indicator Is Flashing One" was published in *Barron's* in the December 9, 1974, issue, which was sent to press on December 6, the exact bottom date for the Dow. The article contrasted the market of 1929 with the market of 1974.

Dan saw a variety of fundamental and technical indicators that presaged a bottom in the stock market. On a fundamental basis, Dan noted that, "since 1929, the Gross National Product had jumped 1,400%, from $103 billion to $1.4 trillion, but at 577.60, the Dow was only 51.5% above its level 43 years earlier, a gain that hardly reflected the tremendous growth in the U.S.

economy." Moreover, valuation levels, investor psychology, and a variety of technical indicators were all signaling a market bottom. In October 1929, the price-to-earnings (P/E) ratio on the Dow was 20.3, triple the 1974 multiple of 6.5. Finally, he noted that at the time, "the overall business outlook is so bleak," that "panic has frightened the last short-term trader into selling." Dan, like Yale, realized, "there is nowhere to go but up."

The ingredients of the 1974 low are not in place today. At $14.9 trillion, the gross national product (GNP) is up tenfold from 1974, while the Dow (roughly 11,500 at the time of writing) is up about twentyfold—the inverse of 1974. In recent years, the Dow has been outpacing the underlying economy.

The Dow's P/E ratio is less attractive at 14.5 today than at the 1974 low of 6.5. Dow earnings plunged during the 2007–2009 financial crisis, going negative for a few quarters in 2007 and 2008, which drove the P/E ratio extremely high. A similar pattern occurred in the 1930s: After earnings went negative in 1932, the Dow P/E remained in double digits until the late 1940s when the P/E hit single digits for three years with a low of 7.7 in 1948 just before the post-WWII boom took off.

Interestingly, the P/E was also in single digits from 1977 to 1981 with a low of 6.4 in 1979. The Dow bounced along in a trading range as earnings picked up until liftoff in 1982. I suspect a similar pattern—the Dow marking time in a trading range while profits rise over the next several years—will bring P/E values back down to more attractive levels as occurred between 1974 and 1982. In short, when the P/E hits single digits again, that will be a signal that the next super boom is ready to explode.

On January 3, 2000, Dan wrote the coda to "Buy Signal," a *Barron's* article aptly titled "Sell Signal." Again, Dan was right on the money. The Dow hit an all-time high the week following the article. The index then shed almost 2,000 points, 16.4 percent to be precise, to a low of 9,796.03 on March 7. Nasdaq took its turn by topping out at 5,048.62 on March 10 and declining to 3,164.55, losing 37.3 percent of its value in just

74 days. All told, over the next two years during the dot-com bust, both indexes lost about 4,000 points at the October 2002 low, with the Dow down 37.8 percent and Nasdaq plummeting 77.9 percent. What Dan accomplished with his long-term predictions pales in comparison with his daily trading abilities. For both his "Buy Signal" and "Sell Signal" *Barron's* articles, and for his success in real market trading during tough volatile markets, we dedicated the *2001 Stock Trader's Almanac* to Dan Turov as well as calling him "Supertrader of the Year and of the Millennium."

But most important, for this book at least, was Dan's May 21, 2001, *Barron's* piece entitled "Mixed Message." In this piece, where the quotation at the beginning of this chapter comes from, he outlines why he "expects to see Dow 10,000 for a long, long time." Dan perceptively observed that the market would:

> Encounter many, many more ledges before the market's long-term swoon ends. And each time it does, a smaller and smaller number of bulls will feed the bear with fresh money. When the bulls stop asking, "Is this the bottom?" and instead are explaining to their friends why "this time it's different, and the market really is a bottomless pit," then it will be time for me to pen "Buy Signal, Part 2." But we're a long way from that. Just how long? I'm not comfortable arguing the bear case; indeed, I was a bull for 25 years. As soon as my "quantification-of-emotions" data signal that the bear market is over, I'll be delighted to argue the bull case again. But the present preponderance of evidence indicates that's far off.
>
> The Dow first reached the 100 level in January 1906. It traded above and below that level for more than 36 years; it wasn't until May 1942 that the market left 100 behind for the last time.
>
> The Industrial Average first reached 1,000 in February 1966. It traded above and below that level for the next

17 years, leaving that figure behind for the last time in February 1983. The Dow first reached the 10,000 level in March 1999. Considering the unprecedented gains of the past several years, would it be that unusual for this benchmark to take a decade or even two before leaving 10,000 in the dust for the last time?

Nine years later the Dow continues to trade above and below 10,000.

In his latest daily e-mail to subscribers, Dan maintains his position from nine years ago: "The super-long-term perspective for the stock market remains bearish (as it has been since January 2000 after having been bullish from December 1974 until then). When the current cyclical bull market ends, expect another nasty crash to perhaps finally bring an end to the long-term bear market that began in 2000." The new Hirsch and the old Turov are on the same page again.

We cite Dan's long-term predictions in order to provide context to the fundamental events that impacted the market over the last decade. Dan, of course, had no way of knowing about the War on Terror, the financial crisis, or the Great Recession. Nonetheless, his view that the market would trade around the 10,000 level for a long period of time was exactly right.

Dot-Com Bust versus 1929 Crash

March 2009 may have brought new lows to old-school market indexes like the Dow and the S&P 500, but that was not the case for the tech-laden Nasdaq that nowadays often provides a better representation of the economy and stock market than its blue-chip brethren. In both 1929 and 2000, a speculative bubble burst and a punishing crash lasting nearly three years took place. Except in 2000, Nasdaq bore the brunt of the carnage while the stodgy, mostly dividend-paying Dow stocks

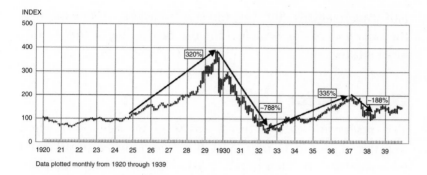

FIGURE 2.1   Dow Monthly High/Low, 1920–1940
Source: Kenneth Safian.

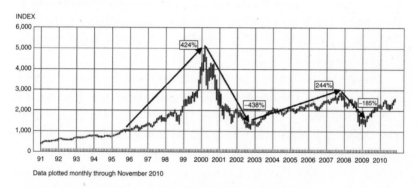

FIGURE 2.2   Nasdaq Monthly High/Low, 1991–2010
Source: Kenneth Safian.

held up better, falling only 37.8 percent from January 2000 to October 2002, compared with the 89.2 percent pounding the Dow took after the 1929 debacle in Figure 2.1. In 2000, dot-coms and wireless stocks, plus the few unscrupulous companies using accounting witchcraft, drove Nasdaq down 77.9 percent in Figure 2.2, almost matching the 1929 decline in the Dow.

As for duration, the 999 days ending in 2002 on the ninth of bear-killer October is just a month short of the length of the 1929 decline. The Dow received its comeuppance from 2007 to 2009 when all the major averages were cut by more than half. But Nasdaq's 2002 low was not breached, indicating that the wartime-secular bear low for the beginning of the twenty-first century is in.

War on Terror

The onset of the war on terror was September 11, 2001, when the World Trade Center and the Pentagon were attacked by terrorists. On October 7, 2001, U.S. forces attacked terrorist strongholds in Afghanistan. Air bombardment of Iraq started on March 20, 2003, and shortly thereafter U.S. forces marched into Baghdad to overthrow Saddam Hussein. President Bush announced "Mission accomplished" in May 2003, but the Iraq War continued as various Iraqi factions fought for power.

Nevertheless, stocks rallied with the Dow gaining 43.5 percent from the October 9, 2002, midterm year low to the preelection-year high on the last day of 2003 (see Figure 2.3). The Nasdaq jumped 50.0 percent in 2003, keeping intact the pattern of gains in preelection years since 1939. As the war dragged on over the next two years, the Dow held the line at 10,500.

Then the credit and housing bubble inflated on equal parts of deregulation, lax oversight, predatory lending practices, and shadow banking. The bubble helped drive the market to new highs. But when the bubble popped, so did the stock market.

The Housing Bubble

The housing market was at the heart of the financial crisis. The inflation and subsequent bursting of the housing bubble was a seminal event in the history of Wall Street and will be a topic analyzed and debated for generations. Let's put it in perspective. Bubbles are usually self-evident in retrospect. It is easy to

Global War on Terror begins Terrorists attack United States 9/11/2001
1 10/7/2001 The American attack on Afganistan begins
2 11/12/2001 Taliban forces abandon Kabul
3 7/5/2002 Iraq rejects UN weapons inspections proposals
4 10/2/2002 Congress authorizes the use of force in Iraq
5 10/12/2002 Terrorists bombs in two nightclubs in Bali
6 10/16/2002 Pres Bush signs the Iraq war resolution
7 3/19/2003 First American bombs dropped on Iraq
8 3/20/2003 Land troops invade Iraq
9 4/9/2003 US forces seize control of Baghdad
10 5/1/2003 Pres Bush proclaims Mission Accomplished
11 12/13/2003 Saddam Hussein is captured in Tikrit
12 2/6/2004 Suicide bomber attacks metro station in Moscow
13 3/11/2004 Coordinated bombings in Madrid kill 191
14 4/4/2004 Fighting breaks out in Najaf, Sadr City, and Basra
15 11/2/2004 President Bush defeats Senator John Kerry
16 7/7/2005 Terrorists strike London's public transit

17 7/11/2006 209 killed in Mumbai train bombings
18 1/10/2007 Iraq troop surge announced
19 4/11/2007 Algerian PM HQ attacked
20 10/18/2007 Former PM Bhutto motocade attacked, 139 killed
21 3/16/2008 Bear Stearns sold to JP Morgan Chase for $2/share
22 9/6/2008 Fannie and Fredie Mac placed in conservatorship
23 9/15/2008 Lehman Brothers files bankruptcy
24 9/16/2008 AIG bailed out by Fed
25 10/3/2008 TARP signed into law
26 11/4/2008 Democrat Barack Obama defeats Senator John McCain
27 11/26/2008 Coordinated attacks span 3 days in Mumbai
28 2/17/2009 17000 additional troop to Afghanistan announced
29 2/27/2009 Iraq troop withdrawal announced
30 6/12/2009 General Motors files bankruptcy
31 12/12/2009 30,000 more troops to be sent to Afghanistan
32 5/1/2010 Times Square bombing attempt thwarted
33 7/25/2010 90k classified war documents posted online at Wikileaks

FIGURE 2.3   Dow During War on Terror

quantify the tech bubble—the Nasdaq rocketed to 5,048, then crashed to 1,114—Figure 2.2 says it all. The housing situation was not as cut and dried. There was no high-profile metric to gauge the relative level of housing prices.

The housing bubble formed for several reasons. Some contend that the origin was the overly aggressive monetary policy in the wake of 9/11 where the Fed's target rate was held at ridiculously low levels (under 2 percent) for the better part of three years. Others point to nefarious lending practices and a gullible populace. Reality is somewhere in between. Greed, hubris, irresponsibility, and foolishness on the part of the lenders and the borrowers were huge factors. Despite the propensity to lay blame on financial institutions, it all does not fall on Wall Street and the banks. No one forced people to buy houses they could not afford. No one made homeowners treat their houses like live-in ATMs. This country was founded on a strong fiscal ethic of saving; we all lost our way!

But what is it going to take to fix a problem that most people couldn't identify until it was too late? What will the recovery look like? Until the housing market is fixed, the economy is in hot water. The magnitude of the damage was far beyond what anyone envisioned. In my view, four key pieces of housing data will help us know when the crisis has passed: existing home sales, housing starts, new home sales, and the National Association of Home Builders' (NAHB) Housing Market Index (HMI).

Existing Home Sales

Existing home sales are the single most important piece of data in our analysis. It is a measure of the ease in which one can buy and sell a house and reflects the relative value that your house has. The massive crescendo in 2006 is indicative of just how out of whack the market got. Not only were people buying houses that they couldn't afford, but individuals were flipping houses for a quick buck. When seven million houses were changing hands each year, something was

FIGURE 2.4   Existing Home Sales
Data source: National Association of Realtors via Economy.com.

wrong. As the indicator peaked in 2005—the height of the bubble—alarms should have been ringing on Pennsylvania Avenue.

As you can see from Figure 2.4, existing home sales were relatively stable until 1996. There were swings, but they were minor. A family home is a long-term investment, and in good times with more people climbing higher on the economic ladder, home sales will tend to rise. That's natural.

After falling dramatically in the financial crisis, existing home sales leveled off recently. Still, we are far from out of the woods. Many homes sold at considerable losses or were foreclosed upon. This number has vacillated wildly since its 2005 peak with a downward trend. Sales spiked in 2009 and again in 2010 on home buyer tax credits, but those credits have since expired. When existing homes sales finally stabilize in a realistic range, the bottom should be set.

Housing Starts

Housing starts indicate how builders feel about the housing market and are important for two reasons. First, home building provides a lot of jobs. When new home building sours, whole construction crews are out of work, not to mention workers in industries that supply building materials. Second, housing starts are a leading indicator of the amount of risk that the market is willing to take. In a good market, home builders ramp up construction in anticipation of future sales. When the market turns, they quickly rein in their plans. As you can see from Figure 2.5, from the housing bottom in 1991 to the top in 2006, housing starts jumped from under 800,000 to over 2.27 million on an annualized basis, a number not seen since 1972. Since the top, the number of housing starts crumbled back below 500,000 in 2009 and is currently looking for support above that level. This is a function of weak demand and lack of credit availability. With a frozen credit market, builders cannot borrow money to buy land and materials and

FIGURE 2.5 Housing Starts
Source: Census Bureau via Economy.com.

finance payroll. Rising housing starts will be one of the first indicators to foreshadow the recovery.

New Home Sales

It takes longer to build a house than sell a house, resulting in a buildup of inventory. Home builders attempt to strike a balance and plan their new construction accordingly. As you can see from Figure 2.6, new home sales fell off a cliff during the financial crisis, down 80 percent, from almost 1.4 million

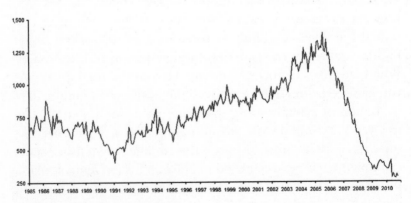

FIGURE 2.6 New Home Sales
Source: Census Bureau via Economy.com.

units to 280,000 in five years. The glut of new homes continues to depress home prices and restrict new construction jobs. New home sales will be the last indicator to turn, but will provide an important confirmation when the housing market turns.

NAHB Housing Market Index

The National Association of Home Builders' Housing Market Index (HMI) may be the best indicator for judging the overall health of the housing market. The HMI was ahead of the curve in forecasting the imminent demise of the market. As you can see in Figure 2.7, from 2005 to 2006, the HMI leveled off and turned down well before the other data began to crumble. The HMI will also convey any optimism within the industry before the data confirm a recovery. Numbers above 50 are a positive bias, below 50, negative. The index has hovered below 20 since 2007. Upticks over the past two years have been encouraging, but have proved fleeting. The big swings have been fake outs, showing that the HMI cannot be looked at in a vacuum. Nonetheless, it is an early warning for swings in the housing market in both directions. It is a number that should be monitored closely.

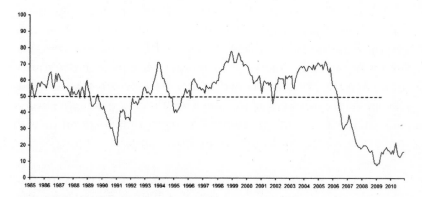

FIGURE 2.7   Housing Market Index
Source: National Association of Home Builders via Economy.com.

Epic damage was done to the economy. It is going to take a concerted effort to repair it and instill confidence among home builders, banks, and the American public. Housing led us down the primrose path and it will also help lead us out of this mess. Monitor these four numbers closely and you will have a good idea of where the economy (and the market) are, and more importantly where they are going. Until housing recovers there is no chance for a meaningful or sustainable bull market to emerge.

Four Horsemen of the Economy

Difficult and protracted issues challenge the leadership of the United States. The War on Terror; Iraq and Afghanistan; the housing and credit crises; the decay of our once great infrastructure; our shamefully expensive, yet inefficient health care system—all plague our still great country and society. Each must be dealt with, but the paramount topic, the one that will cascade throughout the entire globe, is: What is to become of the great American economy? The engine that has fueled the globe since the Second World War is in dire need of an overhaul.

Considerable pressure from both the electorate and the media will continue to be applied to our elected officials until their economic policies show signs of re-igniting growth and employment. Despite monetary and fiscal stimulus in response to the Great Recession, the economy remains in a funk. Clearly, Americans remain unhappy with the status quo. After a prosperous two and a half decades we are on the precipice of regressing back to the not-so-super seventies. If the economy continues to sour, new leadership will be installed in Washington on both ends of Pennsylvania Avenue.

There is no shortage of dire economic predictions for the United States. There are also many well-respected economists who are optimistic about the future. Ultimately, either current policy will be sufficient with a tweak here and there to restart the economy, or persistent underperformance will necessitate a major revamping of economic policy.

To keep tabs on the economy, we devised a simple methodology: the Four Horsemen of the Economy. Individually they indicate different aspects of strength in the U.S. economy; collectively they may provide a rather complete picture.

The Dow

While even the most ardent Dow theorist would confess the index is not without its limitations, it is nonpareil as a barometer for gauging the health of corporate America. True, the S&P is far broader and, thanks to constant rebalancing, better reflects current trends. And the Nasdaq is a much better indicator of innovation and growth. But when the Dow is doing well, America is doing well; when the Dow is in a funk, it not only ripples throughout Wall Street, but Main Street as well.

As of late 2010, the Dow is at new recovery highs and on pace for more gains as a combination of presidential cycle forces, increased corporate profits, a slightly improved economy, and weak investment alternatives are poised to drive the Dow to test the old highs (see Figure 2.8). We expect the Dow to push into the 13,000 to 14,000 range in the first six months of 2011 before it buckles under the weight of the other four horsemen of the economy (and additional economic, corporate, and geopolitical setbacks) into another bear market.

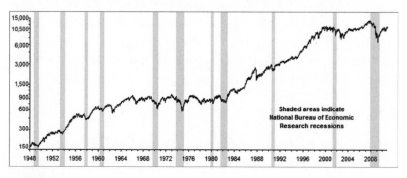

FIGURE 2.8   Dow Jones Industrials (Log Scale) and Recessions 1948–12/10/2010

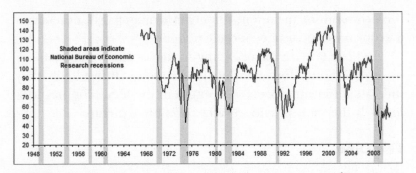

FIGURE 2.9   Consumer Confidence (1985 = 100) and Recessions 1967–12/10/2010
Source: The Conference Board.

To be clear, we do not expect the Dow to produce its average 50 percent gain (since 1914) from the midterm low (in this case, 2010) to the preelection year high (2011) in the current presidential cycle. But a 30–40 percent move from the low of 9,686.48 on July 2, 2010, to a high in 2011 of 13,000–14,000 is quite possible.

Consumer Confidence

The consumer confidence number is essentially a measure of how the great American middle class feels about the economy (see Figure 2.9). The middle class in this country has been squeezed for the better part of the last two decades. Consumer confidence is all about perception and expectations. It is a referendum on the economy of Main Street. The burst of stimulus has helped rejuvenate confidence, but current historically low readings indicate U.S. consumers remain fatigued and strapped for cash. Retail spending has picked up, but from severely depressed levels. Until the Con-Con index heads back up toward the dotted line at 90, as it did in the early 1980s, we do not expect a sustainable recovery.

Inflation

Inflation hits American small to mid-sized business owners and the little guy hardest. Small business owners are the backbone of this country's economy. Small businesses employ tens of millions of Americans. If small businesses are not doing well, it spills over to huge swaths of the populace. Inflation raises costs on small businesses, reducing their ability to expand and hire more workers.

Sustained levels of super high inflation have always created economic problems. Extreme deflation is also an economic depressant. According to the Federal Reserve's latest monetary policy statement on December 14, 2010, "Longer-term inflation expectations have remained stable, but measures of underlying inflation have continued to trend downward." However, as indicated by our six-month exponential moving average of the year-over-year percent changes of the Producer Price Index (PPI) and the Consumer Price Index (CPI), inflation is on the rise (see Figure 2.10). At this juncture of the recovery this is good thing, as it signals rising demand.

At some point inflation will need to abate or the economy will overheat. That is not likely to happen for many years, but it will at some point down the line as it has in the past. Like everything else the Fed and other economic policy makers are not perfect and will likely overshoot on accommodative monetary policy as they have in the past. The big Fed policy dissenter, Thomas Hoenig, head of the Kansas City Fed, accurately pointed out in a *New York Times* interview on December 6, 2010, that "by understandably wanting to see things move more quickly, we create the conditions

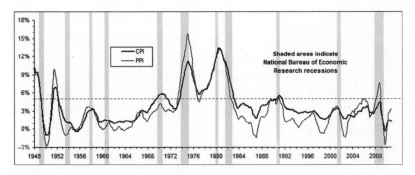

FIGURE 2.10   CPI and PPI 6-Month Exponential Moving Average Year-Over-Year Percent Change
Data source: Bureau of Labor Statistics.

for repeating the mistakes of the past." But in defense of the Bernanke Fed, the lag and complexity of the data make it difficult to perfectly time changes in monetary policy.

Unemployment

Unemployment is the ultimate measure of middle-class economic comfort (see Figure 2.11). In times of economic instability, unemployment seeps all the way to upper management, creating real distress among the jobless and anxiety among those still holding jobs. In the Great Recession, the jobs situation unraveled to a level not seen since the double-dip recession days of the early 1980s. But it is not simply the absolute employment level that is important; it is the direction of the trend that matters most in regard to middle-class confidence in the economy. Not until we see a sustained retreat in unemployment will the economy be on the path to real recovery and higher growth rates.

Colt of the Economy: Jobless Claims Signal

In protracted, long-term bear markets (such as we have been in since 2000), job creation is the linchpin of recovery. The official unemployment rate is a lagging indicator, peaking on average nine months after the end of the bear market and on occasion a year or more later.

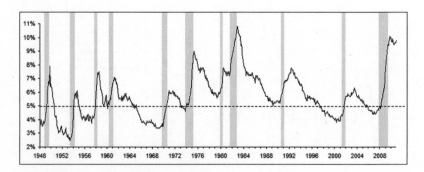

FIGURE 2.11   Unemployment Rate
Data source: Bureau of Labor Statistics.

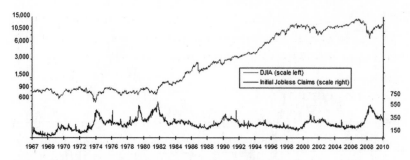

FIGURE 2.12 Dow against Jobless Claims Since 1967
Source: StockTradersAlmanac.com, Department of Labor via Economy.com.

A better indicator is Initial Jobless Claims, a weekly gauge that cuts out much of the government's statistical shenanigans and simply measures folks filing for unemployment insurance for the first time. In Figure 2.12, the Dow's recessionary bear market bottoms fall within two months of the peak in Initial Jobless Claims, except for one instance. Since 1967, Initial Jobless Claims peaked on average about one month after the bear market bottom during a recession. Only the October 1990 bottom induced by Iraq's invasion of Kuwait had Initial Jobless Claims peaking more than two months later. Claims topped out five months later in March 1991 when coalition forces ousted Saddam's forces from Kuwait. The reversal in the number of Initial Jobless Claims since 2009 has been a welcome sign. It indicates the bear market is over and the continued retreat shows an economy on the mend. But this metric can be prone to spikes, as it was during the long recovery from 1974 to 1984.

We Are Not There Yet

The low point of the economy and the bottom of the stock market appear to be behind us. But other factors have yet to align. The CPI has risen just 23 percent since October 2001 (Figure 2.13). President Obama has begun to tack to the

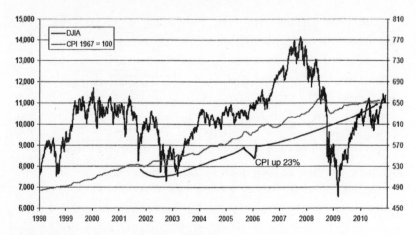

FIGURE 2.13 Dow and CPI, 1998–2010
Sources: Stock Trader's Almanac; www.bls.gov.

center, but we have yet to see him exhibit unwavering leadership and inspire the country. If the new Republican leadership in Congress and the White House can't get the country rolling again, new leaders with new ideas will be elected in the years ahead.

Since the birth of the United States of America, the first truly representational government and free market country in history, the world has been on an increasingly stable path of growth, peace, equal rights, and justice. We have learned to stabilize the swings of expansion and contraction, speculation and investment, innovation and growth and international power struggles. True, these have been crazy times. The super boom of all time in the 1980s and 1990s was followed by 9/11, a protracted war on several fronts, asset and debt bubbles, financial crises, market crashes (flash and otherwise), and the Great Recession. But by my reckoning, the Great Recession has been better than past demises. I have not had to wait in a gasoline line in the twenty-first century on odd-and-even-license-plate-rationing days as I did as a child in late 1973 and early 1974, and again in 1979.

The 1982 to 2000 super boom was one of a kind, powered by baby-boomer consumerism and incredible technological advancement. It will be a hard act to follow. The post–World War I and World War II booms were warm-up acts. There was no baby boom to power them, but waves of immigrants helped create plenty of demand and an appetite for a better life through new ideas and hard work.

Many of the innovations of the 1980s and 1990s were spawned in the first 80 years of the twentieth century and earlier. But nonetheless, the breakthroughs of previous generations took the economy, society, and stocks to new heights. The future may look bleak now, but as J. D. Rockefeller accurately said in July 1932 on his 93rd birthday, "Depressions have come and gone. Prosperity has always returned and will again."

We have experienced economic and fiscal challenges before, and we will ride out of our current problems on the back of political stability, reduced global violence, inflation, human ingenuity, and the zest for life! Depression appears to have been averted with no dark ages in sight. Geopolitical challenges, war, drought, famine, and atrocities persist, but we have managed to avoid another world war, depression, or thermonuclear disaster. We have come a long way and we have further to go.

THE FORTUNE TELLERS

Mystics, prophets, visionaries, and prognosticators have captured the imaginations and ire of the masses and critics for millennia. From Mesopotamia to Mesoamerica, soothsayers forecasted the demise of civilization and the coming of messiahs. According to the Mayan Long Count Calendar, the world that they calculated started on August 11, 3114 BCE now is scheduled to end on Triple-Witching Day, December 21, 2012.

In reality, this is more than likely the end of a cycle based on Mayan dating methodology. Nostradamus' quatrains supposedly predicted everything from natural disasters to the Ottoman invasions of Europe to the 9/11 attacks. Most of the forecasts were revealed in hindsight, however, after careful interpretation of his writings.

By nature financial analysis involves quite a bit of prognostication. What good would the analysis be if it did not project the future for the analyzed security, company, sector, or market as a whole? Without some sort of price or time target or valuation metric, the discussion of the pros and cons of any given financial instrument or market is rendered rather useless. But this is not license to make extremely long-term predictions.

The Super Boom forecast is a continuation of a constant process of projecting where the stock market is headed over the next several months and years. I grew up during the culmination of my father's accurate prediction of a 500 percent move from the 1974 low, and I have been studying, retooling, and fine-tuning the Hirsch method for years in search of the next boom.

Economists, Wall Street analysts, money managers, traders, and individual investors forecast the market constantly. Some do it throughout the day out of habit or occupational obligation; others on a daily, weekly, or monthly basis. Annual forecasts are a rite of passage on the Street, but long-term prognostications that project major price swings decades out are reserved for only the most enterprising market forecasters.

In any case, many forecasts, both accurate and erroneous, historical and current, exist. In an effort to add some perspective to my super boom prediction, I examine in this part a few of the most famous market fortunes ever told (or sold), as well as those fortunes still being written.

CHAPTER 3

The History of Ignorance and the Ignorance of History

It is wise to remember that too much success [in the stock market] is in itself an excellent warning.

—Gerald M. Loeb
The Battle for Investment Survival

In the 66th episode of the early 1970s classic sitcom, *The Odd Couple,* Felix and Oscar are mistakenly arrested for scalping a ticket to a Broadway show. Felix, serving as their lawyer, later cross-examines the woman who tried to offer him money for the ticket. Felix asks the woman if he ever said he was selling the ticket. The woman says, "I just assumed."

Felix interrupts her, asking for the courtroom blackboard to be wheeled out. He argues his and Oscar's innocence by circling three sections of the word assume. This infamous lesson, that when you assume you make an *ass* out of *u* and *me,* is especially applicable to the market.

Investors and traders know better than anyone that assumptions are dangerous. A company you assumed was honest turns out to have fraudulent bookkeeping. A trend you assumed would continue reverses. Market assumptions and assumptions about valuation are particularly risky, especially when used to predict the future. Many forecasters have lost their shirts as well their reputations by betting on erroneous assumptions.

We at the Hirsch Organization believe what has been is the best indicator of what will be. We believe the future is informed by the past; that investor behavior and market behavior move in synchronized cycles; that looking closely at history can tell us what to expect in the future. In light of my prediction that the Dow will reach 38,820 by 2025, it makes sense to first reflect on other bold predictions, in times past and present, both salient and foolhardy. In this chapter, I explore one such famous prediction to give context to my own.

When You Assume

In the annual *Stock Trader's Almanac,* I highlight the best investment books of the year. Only books that are released after the last edition of the *Almanac* was published or whose advance reading copies are sent to us for review by the publishers are considered. Our intention is to bring to the attention of our readers the timeliest and most useful tactics and strategies, as well as works that reveal new, valuable insight into what makes the markets tick or the world go 'round.

In 1999, James K. Glassman and Kevin A. Hassett's *Dow 36,000* was published to much hullabaloo. We reviewed it. While these two gentlemen are of highly regarded stock and their thesis heavily researched, documented, and detailed, it was intentionally omitted from our perennial list of titles. The forecast, made in 1999, that the Dow would reach 36,000 in the next three to five years did not come to pass.

Dow 36,000

Glassman and Hassett are Ivy Leaguers with impressive curriculum vitae, including extensive published works and articles prior to *Dow 36,000* and since. They've won awards, held stints in government, and maintain affiliations with renowned public policy think tanks, such as the American Enterprise Institute. Glassman graduated cum laude from Harvard with a B.A. in government. He has been a financial columnist for *The Washington Post* and *Reader's Digest*, and written for a host of publications. He was the publisher of *The New Republic*, president of *The Atlantic Monthly*, and executive vice president of *U.S. News & World Report*. He moderated CNN's Capital Gang and hosted PBS's TechnoPolitics. A list of his accolades and accomplishments seems to go on interminably. After serving on the U.S. government's Advisory Board on Public Diplomacy in the Arab and Muslim World in 2003 and as chairman of the Broadcasting Board of Governors in 2007, he became the Under Secretary for Public Diplomacy and Public Affairs in the Bush administration in 2008.

Kevin A. Hassett has a B.A. in economics from Swarthmore and a Ph.D. in economics from the University of Pennsylvania. Neither as prolific as Glassman nor as flamboyant, Hassett has written articles in major newspapers like *The New York Times*, *The Wall Street Journal*, *National Review*, and is now a columnist for Bloomberg News. He has also written several books on economics and finance. Hassett has been an economics professor at Columbia, an economist at the Federal Reserve Board of Governors, a consultant to the Treasury Department under the George H. W. Bush and Clinton administrations, as well as chief economic advisor to John McCain (of self-admittedly dubious economic prowess) in the 2000 presidential primary and an economic advisor to McCain's presidential election campaign in 2008. Hassett also advised the George W. Bush reelection campaign in 2004.

Despite these lengthy resumes, Glassman and Hassett failed to remember and respect the lessons of history. Even

Helicopter Ben Bernanke, whose nickname is derived from his reference to Milton Friedman's comment that deflation could be fought by dropping money out of a helicopter, has his feet firmly planted in history as he tries to ensure we do not make the same monetary mistakes of the Great Depression and Japan's Lost Decade(s) by tightening the monetary spigot too soon or too much. Glassman and Hassett cited some of the same historical market moves as I do for my forecast, such as the super boom from 1982 to 2000. But they failed to remember other equally relevant and important bits of history: the sideways market of 1966–1982, the tendencies of humanity and business to swing from peace to war and boom to bust when least expected, and the general cyclicality of the market.

They assumed the market of the 18-year super bull leading up to 1999 was going to be the market of the future. They assumed that stocks would reap double-digit gains, averaging 24.7 percent for the Dow, as it had for five years from 1995 to 1999. In their view, the market could not possibly have been on the verge of another extended secular bear market where U.S. equities would gain little ground for the next 10 or 20 years. Stocks were on a clear path to their "perfectly reasonable price or PRP," the phrase and acronym repeated throughout the book ad nauseum, and would not stop until the risk premium of stocks equaled that of bonds, and dividend yields neared zero as investors came to their senses and ceased assessing stocks with more risk than bonds. Average historic growth rates over the previous 50 to 100 years (and beyond) of corporate revenue and dividends would continue unabated, despite several instances over that time frame of major disruption. The steady decline in dividend yields and increase in price-to-earnings ratios was unstoppable, and the stock market gains of the late 1990s were set to continue straight on through to Dow 36,000 in "early 2005."[1] Even the laws of physics ceased to apply, as what went up did not come down.

---

[1] James K. Glassman and Kevin A. Hassett, *Dow 36,000* (New York: Times Books, 1999), 140.

Glassman and Hassett were convinced that nothing could derail the market's ascension to unprecedented valuations. But trends have never continued uninterrupted for such a sustained period of time. Often at precisely the moment a market seems unstoppable, it stops.

This is, of course, precisely what happened. From just about the time the authors sent the book to press in mid-1999, stock dividend payouts for the S&P 500 peaked and declined for the next two years. Risk returned to the stock market in dangerous and dramatic fashion as the speculative bubble of the dot-com era collapsed. Bond payouts retreated in tandem. Stocks went nowhere. Dividend yields crept higher and bond yields declined during the economic contraction.

From 2003 to 2007, payouts and yields increased while stock prices soared. This proved to be a second bubble, expanded on unsustainable real estate growth, which led to the 2007–2009 financial crisis. The spread between the 10-year Treasury bond and the S&P 500 dividend yield reached parity for the first time since 1962.

The Goldilocks economy was too hot, then too cold. In the face of geopolitical upheaval, war, recession, a contagion of debt, and a crisis of confidence, risk was crowned the new king. In Figure 3.1, the spread between what bonds and stocks pay in 2010 is much closer than in 1999. S&P 500 dividend

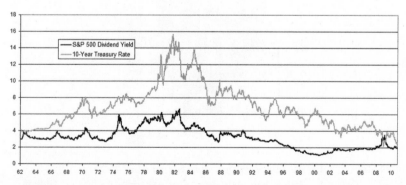

FIGURE 3.1   S&P 500 Dividend Yield and 10-Year Treasury Rate Since 1962

yields are at about 2 percent and the 10-year Treasury is under 3 percent, both indicators of significant risk. Add to that a commodity bull market that appears to be bubbling.

Based on myopic data, Glassman and Hassett made a host of dubious assumptions. The crux of their theory and the quintessential error of their ways was that the steady growth of earnings and dividends stocks had enjoyed in the late 1990s would continue ad infinitum, or until Dow 36,000, and the risk premium of stocks would continue to shrink. In September 1999, as *Dow 36,000* was hitting the bookstores, Glassman and Hassett had a lengthy article in *The Atlantic Monthly* summarizing their theory and forecast (Figure 3.2).

They began their argument for "a one-time-only rise to much higher ground—to the neighborhood of 36,000 for the Dow Jones Industrial Average," reminding readers that stocks had moved up fivefold from 1982 to 1994—the bulk of the 500 percent move my father, Yale Hirsch, accurately forecasted in 1976. They then cited the three years of stellar gains in 1995, 1996, and 1997 when the Dow gained more than 20 percent each year, averaging 27.4 percent per year. The authors

FIGURE 3.2 *The Atlantic Monthly* **Cover, September 1999**
Source: Copyright 2010 The Atlantic.com as published in The Atlantic Online. Distributed by Tribune Media Services.

accurately observed, "Never before in modern history had the market had three years this good in a row."[2] In fact, as the book was hitting the stores 11 years ago, the market was completing a historic five-year run of gains of more than 16 percent each year for the Dow, averaging 24.7 percent per year. We may not have had three years that good in a row, but the five years from 1924 to 1928 averaged 26.7 percent per year with four of the five achieving gains greater than 26 percent per year and only 1926 posted a fractional gain.

From a purely historical perspective, this was probably the worst time to be buying and holding. It took 25 years for the Dow to surpass the 1929 high. Ten years after their prediction, the Dow was still around 10,000.

Dissatisfied with the wisdom of the ages—that the precipitous rise in stock prices was another bout of what Charles Mackay described in his 1841 classic *Extraordinary Popular Delusions and the Madness of Crowds*—Glassman and Hassett embarked on a journey to ascertain the "right value" for stocks by dismissing "P/E ratios and other valuation indicators." Their research to find the holy "perfectly reasonable price or PRP" by way of estimating cash flow convinced them that their theory was correct and that "the rise in stock prices over the past two decades . . . will continue, at least until Dow 36,000."[3]

In their conclusion, the authors flirted with a veiled caveat: "If the risk premium did return to normal, the carnage would be devastating . . . stock prices would have to fall by 75 percent."[4] This is precisely what happened to Nasdaq from March

---

[2]Copyright © 1999 by The Atlantic Monthly Company. All rights reserved. *The Atlantic Monthly;* September 1999; Dow 36,000–99.09; Volume 284, No. 3; pages 37–58.
[3]Copyright © 1999 by The Atlantic Monthly Company. All rights reserved. *The Atlantic Monthly;* September 1999; Dow 36,000–99.09; Volume 284, No. 3; pages 37–58.
[4]Copyright © 1999 by The Atlantic Monthly Company. All rights reserved. *The Atlantic Monthly;* September 1999; Dow 36,000–99.09; Volume 284, No. 3; pages 37–58.

2000 to October 2002. But they saw a "decline in the risk premium as reasonable and long-lasting, not as insane and transitory."[5]

At its most basic level, the Dow 36,000 theory was just buy-and-hold in fancy clothes. "American investors have learned to buy and hold. Over the past few decades investors have entered the stock market the way a cautious child enters cool water."[6] Or perhaps the way a mindless crustacean gently falls asleep as a pot of cold water slowly comes to a boil. The problem is most regular investors get confident at the top and scared at the bottom: a case-in-point argument for market timing and contrarian investing. Buy-and-hold may have been the mantra of the 1990s, when even cabbies had good stock tips, but timing was the saving grace of the 2000s. If we've learned anything from Glassman and Hassett, it's that all things are cyclical, and buy and hold will have its place again with the rise of the next super boom.

Your Money Where Your Mouth Is

On November 14, 2004, on *Meet the Press*, political pundit and strategist James Carville cracked a raw egg on his face saying, "I've got egg on my face. It was a bad prediction.... When you come on Sunday morning TV and you make a prediction and, you know, you're that far off, then you've got egg on your face."

In March of that year, Russert had convinced Carville to bet $1,000 against Mary Matalin (Carville's wife) on the outcome of the 2004 election. The winnings would go to the Boys & Girls Clubs of Greater Washington. In November, covered in egg, Carville pulled out his checkbook.

---

[5]Copyright © 1999 by The Atlantic Monthly Company. All rights reserved.
The Atlantic Monthly; September 1999; Dow 36,000–99.09; Volume 284, No. 3; pages 37–58.
[6]Copyright © 1999 by The Atlantic Monthly Company. All rights reserved.
The Atlantic Monthly; September 1999; Dow 36,000–99.09; Volume 284, No. 3; pages 37–58.

Glassman and Hassett made $1,000 bets as well. *The Atlantic Monthly* received and published several astute and colorful retorts in the January 2000 issue. One was from the venerable James Stack, president of InvesTech Research. From his perch in Whitefish, Montana, the prudent Stack quickly tore down Glassman and Hassett's theory, showing the inherent flaws in their logic that "a normal bond and a growth bond are equivalent in present value if the sum of the growth bond's interest rate plus its growth rate is equal to the normal bond's interest rate."[7]

The bond growth they estimated, "must occur in bond *principal* each year ... not simply in interest-rate payout, as the authors mistakenly assume."[8] Stack pointed out that a 0.5 percent growth bond with a 9.5 percent annual increase "cannot have the same present value as a normal bond yielding 10 percent (0.5 percent + 9.5 percent), because it would require 34 years before the increasing yield of the growth bond matched the yield of the normal bond. Of course, total return would not be equivalent for many years after that (owing to 34 years of less than 10 percent yield in the growth bond)."[9]

Another reader, J. Douglas Van Sant, a lawyer from Stockton, CA, wrote, "I would be willing to bet Glassman and Hassett that even 10 years from now, when earnings and dividends should have nearly doubled, the Dow Jones Industrial Average will still be closer to its current level of 11,000 than to their hyperbolic projection of 36,000."[10]

The authors replied to Van Sant that "if the Dow is closer to 10,000 than to 36,000 10 years from now, we will each

---

[7] *The Atlantic Monthly;* January 2000; Letters to the Editor–00.01; Volume 285, No. 1; pages 6–17.
[8] *The Atlantic Monthly;* January 2000; Letters to the Editor–00.01; Volume 285, No. 1; pages 6–17.
[9] *The Atlantic Monthly;* January 2000; Letters to the Editor–00.01; Volume 285, No. 1; pages 6–17.
[10] *The Atlantic Monthly;* January 2000; Letters to the Editor–00.01; Volume 285, No. 1; pages 6–17.

give \$1,000 to the charity of your choice."[11] I recently called Mr. Van Sant. He informed me that the authors made good on their bet and pointed me to the follow-up in the May 2010 issue of *The Atlantic Monthly*, reprinted here.

Dow Loses Points, but Reader Wins 10-Year-Old Bet

More than 10 years ago in these pages, James K. Glassman and Kevin A. Hassett argued a new theory of stock valuation, writing that the Dow Jones Industrial Average would rise "to the neighborhood of 36,000" (*"Dow 36,000,"* September 1999 *Atlantic*). In January 2000, J. Douglas Van Sant of Stockton, California, wrote in to say that their theory was "a giant fallacy." He bet Glassman and Hassett that in 10 years, the Dow would be closer to 11,000. The writers agreed to the bet: "If the Dow is closer to 10,000 than to 36,000 ten years from now, we will each give \$1,000 to the charity of your choice."

On December 31, 2009, the Dow closed at 10,428, as Brad W. Bradley of Bel Air, Maryland, pointed out to *Atlantic* editors earlier this year. Glassman and Hassett conceded, donating \$1,000 each to the Salvation Army, by Van Sant's request.

"It's been a bad run for optimists," Hassett noted. "James and I included a chapter in our book [based on the article] outlining why the equity-premium decline that was at the core of our thesis might stop or reverse itself. Just about every equity-downside scenario we could envision, including terrorist attack, later became a reality. Going forward, investors have to decide whether the U.S. has had a run of bad luck or whether something fundamental has changed that cannot be reversed. Either is possible."

"I'm surprised at the way it turned out. I thought their theory was pretty extreme, and that was the point of my letter," Van

---

[11] *The Atlantic Monthly;* January 2000; Letters to the Editor–00.01; Volume 285, No. 1; pages 6–17. Copyright 2010 The Atlantic.com as published in The Atlantic Online. Distributed by Tribune Media Services.

TABLE 3.1 Dow Bulls and Bears Since 1900

Beginning		Ending		Bull		Bear	
Date	DJIA	Date	DJIA	% Gain	Days	% Change	Days
9/24/00	38.80	6/17/01	57.33	47.8%	266	−46.1%	875
11/9/03	30.88	1/19/06	75.45	144.3	802	−48.5	665
11/15/07	38.83	11/19/09	73.64	89.6	735	−27.4	675
9/25/11	53.43	9/30/12	68.97	29.1	371	−24.1	668
7/30/14	52.32	11/21/16	110.15	110.5	845	−40.1	393
12/19/17	65.95	11/3/19	119.62	81.4	684	−46.6	660
8/24/21	63.90	3/20/23	105.38	64.9	573	−18.6	221
10/27/23	85.76	9/3/29	381.17	344.5	2,138	−47.9	71
11/13/29	198.69	4/17/30	294.07	48.0	155	−86.0	813
7/8/32	41.22	9/7/32	79.93	93.9	61	−37.2	173
2/27/33	50.16	2/5/34	110.74	120.8	343	−22.8	171
7/26/34	85.51	3/10/37	194.40	127.3	958	−49.1	386
3/31/38	98.95	11/12/38	158.41	60.1	226	−23.3	147
4/8/39	121.44	9/12/39	155.92	28.4	157	−40.4	959
4/28/42	92.92	5/29/46	212.50	128.7	1,492	−23.2	353
5/17/47	163.21	6/15/48	193.16	18.4	395	−16.3	363
6/13/49	161.60	1/5/53	293.79	81.8	1,302	−13.0	252
9/14/53	255.49	4/6/56	521.05	103.9	935	−19.4	564
10/22/57	419.79	1/5/60	685.47	63.3	805	−17.4	294
10/25/60	566.05	12/13/61	734.91	29.8	414	−27.1	195
6/26/62	535.76	2/9/66	995.15	85.7	1,324	−25.2	240
10/7/66	744.32	12/3/68	985.21	32.4	788	−35.9	539
5/26/70	631.16	4/28/71	950.82	50.6	337	−16.1	209
11/23/71	797.97	1/11/73	1,051.70	31.8	415	−45.1	694
12/6/74	577.60	9/21/76	1,014.79	75.7	655	−26.9	525
2928/78	742.12	9/8/78	907.74	22.3	192	−16.4	591
4/21/80	759.13	4/27/81	1,024.05	34.9	371	−24.1	472
8/12/82	776.92	11/29/83	1,287.20	65.7	474	−15.6	238
7/24/84	1,086.57	8/25/87	2,722.42	150.6	1,127	−36.1	55
10/19/87	1,738.74	7/17/90	2,999.75	72.5	1,002	−21.2	86
10/11/90	2,365.10	7/17/98	9,337.97	294.8	2,836	−19.3	45
8/31/98	7,539.07	1/14/00	11,722.98	55.5	501	−29.7	616
9/21/01	8,235.81	3/19/02	10,635.25	29.1	179	−31.5	204
10/9/02	7,286.27	10/9/07	14,164.53	94.4	1,826	−53.8	517
3/9/09	6,547.05	12/28/10	11,575.54	76.8[*]	659[*]		
			Average	85.7%	755	−31.5%	410

[*]At press time – not in averages.

Based on Dow Jones Industrial Average. 1900–2000.   Date: Ned Davis Research.
The NYSE was closed from 7/31/1914 to 12/11/1914 due to World War I.
DJIA figures were then adjusted back to reflect the composition change from 12 to 20 stock in September 1916.
Source: Stock Trader's Almanac.

Sant said. "I never imagined the Dow would have been less than in 1999 [when it closed the year at 11,453]. In a way, I was probably just as wrong as they were. If someone had bet me it would be lower, I would have taken the bet and lost it. Everybody lost on that one."

The authors' assumption of a new world order for stock valuations and risk premiums was based on an abbreviated history of the financial world. They were likely blinded by the market performance of the immediate years or even of the gains from the great super boom that, we know now, was winding down as they went to press. The Dow had gained ground in each of the nine years from 1991 to 1999. From July 1984 to January 2000, the Dow suffered only three brief bear markets, each lasting less than three months, as you can see in Table 3.1.

On March 8, 2009, in an article for *The Washington Post* titled "Waiting for Dow 36,000," reporter Carlos Lozada asked Glassman, "But you don't feel the need to apologize to someone who read your book, went in and got creamed?"[12]

Glassman responded, "Absolutely not."

---

[12]"OUTSPOKEN: A Conversation with James K. Glassman, Waiting for Dow 36,000," *The Washington Post*, March 8, 2009, B2.

An Argument against Financial Calamity

I would like to say to Milton [Friedman]: regarding the Great Depression, you're right; we did it. We're very sorry. But thanks to you, we won't do it again.

—Ben Bernanke

Where Glassman and Hassett focused on new valuation methods to justify their super boom, Harry S. Dent, Jr., and Robert R. Prechter, Jr., two of the most popular market fortune tellers, rely on social trends, business acumen, and an implicit understanding of history. Dent and Prechter are not academics, journalists, or public policy wonks. Both gentlemen provide constant updates and revisions to their forecasts, make a comfortable living advising clients and readers, and have been humble enough to admit error from time to time and change their outlook accordingly.

Both also share a predominantly negative view of the coming decade. As my view of the next several years is considerably less negative, I'll address in this chapter their arguments and make the best case for a coming era of prosperity, not doom.

A gifted student, Harry Dent graduated first in his class at the University of South Carolina before getting his MBA from Harvard as a Baker Scholar, the top academic award at HBS. In the 1980s, after working as a strategic consultant for a large consulting firm, he ventured out on his own, working with entrepreneurial companies and honing his demographic economic analysis methods. He founded HS Dent in 1987, which provides economic research, forecasting, and advisory services to individuals, financial advisors, and corporations through various periodical publications, special reports, seminars, and speaking engagements. When I reached out to the folks at HS Dent in order to get a better feel for where their thinking was currently at, they graciously provided access.

Dent's father and namesake was an American political strategist and is considered the architect of the Republican Southern Strategy that was crucial to Richard M. Nixon winning the presidential election in 1968.

Robert Prechter graduated from Yale in 1971 with a degree in psychology. He is a Chartered Market Technician who began his professional career in 1975 doing technical market analysis for Merrill Lynch in New York City. He has served as president of the esteemed Market Technicians Association and is a member of three high-IQ organizations: Mensa, Intertel, and the Triple Nine Society. After publishing *Elliott Wave Principle* in 1978, he began publishing his monthly forecasting publication, *The Elliott Wave Theorist*, and has been doing so since. His organization, Elliott Wave International, produces analysis, forecasts, and investment recommendations for stock, bond, currency, and commodity markets across the planet.

The Dent method uses demographic analysis to identify changing cultural patterns and the impact they have had on the economy and asset prices. Prechter is a proponent of social behavior, what he calls *socionomics*, technical stock market analysis, and the Elliott wave principle. There is some symmetry to both gentlemen's work, methodology, and prognostications. Wave theory, cycles, and pattern recognition permeate their work. And Dent utilizes Elliott wave theory as well.

So it should not come as much of a surprise that they've come to similar conclusions about our economic future—that we're headed for the kind of severe market decline not seen since the Great Depression.

The Dent Method

The Dent method is a long-term economic forecasting system based on demographic trends. In order to project major shifts in the economy and financial markets, Dent measures the amount of people who are at their peak spending age in the economy, coming into their peak spending age, or exiting their peak spending age. Dent believes that the massive economic growth we experienced in the 1980s and 1990s in the last super boom were predominately attributed to the massive population growth of the post-WWII baby boom generation spending money in their prime years: raising children, buying houses, consuming technology, and investing.

In *The Great Boom Ahead* (Hyperion, 1993), Dent accurately forecasted in 1993 a tremendous boom based on U.S. baby boom consumer spending that would peter out in 2007 at Dow 8,500. He got the year right, but underestimated the level of the market during the boom. And by many measures the boom actually ended in 2000 with the bursting of the tech bubble.

In 1998, in his book *Roaring 2000s* (Touchstone, 1998), and in his 1999 update of *The Great Boom Ahead,* he overcompensated for the boom at hand and projected the Dow could reach the top of his growth channel of 36,000 to 40,000 by 2010. As the market began to run out of steam in 2006, Dent reduced his forecast to 16,000 to 20,000 for the Dow.

Then in 2008, as the financial crisis and Great Recession were taking hold, Dent came out with his latest book, *The Great Depression Ahead.* This book and forecast picks up on where

The Great Boom Ahead and *The Roaring 2000s* left off. The end of baby boom spending would be the beginning of the next depression that will drive the Dow down to 3,800.

He states, "We have a very high confidence level in forecasting that our economy will worsen and that we will see the worst downturn since the 1930s between mid- to late 2009 and 2012. Whether the Dow falls to 3,800 (our best target) or lower or higher is harder to forecast. And whether the actual bottom comes in late 2010 or mid-2011 or mid- to late 2012 or even late 2014 is also a question mark. Whether unemployment reaches 10 percent or 12 percent or 15 percent or higher is also to be seen."[1] It remains to be seen, but I believe the "downturn" came in 2007–2009.

Dent also touches on the unfavorable geopolitical cycle that plagues the United States every 16 to 18 years. But he does not consider that we have been in one such cycle since 2000. In his November 10, 2010, *HS Dent Forecast* he writes, "This third bear market bubble is projected to lead to a fall in the Dow to approximately 3,000 to 3,300, likely by late 2012 but possibly by late 2014 on our cycles. Such a fall would back up our observations that almost all bubbles go back to where they started from or a little lower. The stock bubble started in late 1994 at 3,800 on the Dow. Thus, we have been expecting 3,800 or lower for an ultimate bottom. The more the bubble grows the more investors get in, which will cause the bubble to fall even further, creating another wave of havoc."

The date 1994 seems rather arbitrary. Maybe this bubble has already gone back to the area of the 1998 bear market low of Dow 7,539? We have been building a long-term base at this level for 12 years with a 2001 low of 8,236 and with brief stints below 7,500 in 2002 to 7,286 and a low in 2009 of 6,547.

Dent is right in his current assessment that inflation will vanish or is at least diminishing. It has for the time being. But Dent

---

[1]Dent, *The Great Depression Ahead,* page 30.

misses that the previous booms were caused in part by inflation and that inflation has always come back faster than anticipated.

I am not convinced that spending peaks at age 46 anymore as Dent continues to believe. People are living longer, marrying later, and having children later. He also may not be accounting for a global baby boom. Spending in China, India, and other emerging countries can compensate for the lack of a baby boom in the United States. Then there is the continuing immigration trend into America, both legal and illegal, that has and will continue to contribute to consumer spending. These other population trends helped drive the previous booms following WWI and WWII. There were no official baby booms back then. Dent does well spotting big trends, but has been admittedly off on the timing and level of the highs and lows.

Conceptually, Dent was and still is quite correct. Unfortunately, he overshot on the level of the Dow. His timing of the peaks and valleys of the many other asset classes for which he has rendered forecasts is not that far off.

In *The Great Depression Ahead*, Dent correctly categorizes the extension of the current economic slump and the continuation of the secular bear market for stocks. But he seems to be marking the beginning of the secular bear cycle at the 2007 top, as opposed to the end of 1999 or early 2000 where I and many others place it. This, I suspect, is part of the reason why his forecast for depression will end up being too deep and too long.

After all, the Dow came nowhere close to Dent's prognostication in *The Roaring 2000s* of 40,000 by 2009, and his latest forecast in *The Great Depression Ahead* and in his current newsletter to subscribers for Dow 3,800 somewhere between late 2012 and late 2014 is just as extreme.

Conquering Prechter's Crash

Prechter has also been on the right side of the market much of the time. His 1978 book, *Elliott Wave Principle*, written with A. J. Frost, accurately predicted the super boom of the 1980s and

1990s. *Conquer the Crash* (Wiley) first came out in mid-2002 just as the second "wave" of the secular bear market that began in January 2000 was gathering momentum. But, and this is a big but, after his prescient call for a bull market of epic dimensions back in 1978 and a warning in October 1987 to get out of stocks before the 1987 Crash on Black Monday, Prechter turned prematurely bearish in the late 1980s. According to the Elliott wave principle, the grand super cycle had peaked and we were in for "the biggest financial catastrophe since the founding of the Republic."

The primary reason for Prechter's forecast of the Dow falling below 1,000 is the Elliot wave structure. But he also cites a monetary reason. "The tremendous inflation of the past 76 years" has been built on credit and "credit can implode."

Prechter believes, "the only monetary outcome that will make sense of the Elliot Wave structure is for ... credit to shrink by 90 percent." He notes the "eroded state of capital goods in the U.S. and the depletion of the manufacturing capacity. ... The future has been fully mortgaged; it's time to pay. But there is no money to pay." He says "purchasing power will disappear" and this will end in "a collapse in the 'money supply.'"

From our vantage point the stock market continues to rally in powerful booms as we show in this book as a direct result of this tremendous inflation. And by his calculations the Dow will also shrink by 90 percent as it did from September 1929 to July 1932.

As I pointed out in Chapter 2, the demise of Nasdaq from 2000 to 2002 matches up well with the Dow's historic meltdown in 1929. You may argue that the Dow was cut to almost a tenth of its 1929 high by the bottom of 1932, while Nasdaq was only reduced to a fifth of its 2000 high by 2002. I would argue that Nasdaq's meteoric rise of nearly 100 times from the 1974 low of 54.87 to the 2000 top of 5,048.17, or the 15-fold move from the 1990 low of 325.44, dwarfs the Dow's 12-fold move from the 1903 low of 30.88 (adjusted) to the top in 1929 of

381.17, or the 6- or 7-fold moves from 1921 (63.90) and 1914 (52.32), respectively. Whatever your argument, the similarities are undeniable (see Figures 2.1 and 2.2).

Though humanity often fails to remember the lessons of history, we have learned and matured on many levels. In particular, we have learned the financial, economic, and political lessons of the Great Depression. In his December 3, 2010, Market Comment, the venerable Don Hays of the eponymous Hays Advisory agrees, noting that "this country was on the verge of another Depression of the same degree as 1929–1932. . . . some special people (Bernanke and Paulson) took the steps (in my opinion) to keep this economy, this financial system, and this country from going that same 1929 path." A drop in the Dow from the recent high of around 11,500 to Dent's 3,800 or Prechter's 1,000 would equate to catastrophic losses of 67 percent and 91 percent, respectively.

I believe that the 2009 intraday low of 6,470 or thereabout will hold as did the previous secular lows of 1974, 1942 (or 1932 depending where you slice it), and 1914. By my calculations we are past the midway point of the secular bear that began in 2000 with the dot-com bust and took hold in 2001 after the 9/11 attacks and the war on terror began. Nasdaq and technology stocks took the heat this cycle, falling 78 percent from 2000 to 2002. It remains at half its all-time highs as of December 2010.

Depression Averted

Dent's and Prechter's forecasts seem at first blush like the words of the overzealous. My forecast came off this way when the press release for the *2011 Almanac* came out in late September 2010. My intention with *Super Boom* is to dispel that notion. I concur with the general concept of restrained economic growth and a lid on stock prices over the next several years. I believe we will flirt with the lower end of the market's range during that time. A test of the lows in the Dow 6,500–7,500 range in the

2012–2014 time frame is entirely in the cards. But Dow 3,800 or 1,000 are not, in my opinion. For that kind of implosion to occur we would have to experience a 1930s-style market collapse or go through a liquidity trap like the Japanese did, followed by another calamitous financial crisis or geopolitical disaster that erases confidence and spooks the market.

It would be cavalier to assume that these are not real possibilities, but they remain outside chances. The market has already suffered its lost decade and it will continue to suffer for several more years. The U.S. Federal Reserve and federal government, along with other central banks, much of the developed world's economic and political leadership, as well as academic and business leaders, seem quite conscious of the events and policies that helped create the Great Depression and Japan's Lost Decades and are doing everything in their power to prevent either of these brutal outcomes.

So far, monetary and fiscal policies have been effective, not perfect, but effective. It will take time to heal, but we are healing, and the next super boom will not be ignited until several factors align, including a properly functioning government that is in synch with the private sector, stimulating innovation and sustainable economic growth. The world is a much flatter place than it was 80 years ago. Protectionist inclinations exist, but central banks, the IMF, the World Bank, and the governments of the major civilized nations of the world exist to prevent sustained economic stagnation.

Dent, Prechter, and I all think we will be in a funk for several years. Dent and Prechter think the market will go lower and take longer to recover. Throughout history, the market has teetered on the brink of collapse, and yet today it remains standing. The Great Recession has the housing market in the sewer and unemployment at its highest level since the infamous double-dip recession of the 1980s. Credit has imploded, but the world has not. Dent focuses on demographic waves, Prechter on Elliott waves, but the real wave is the one built by war and peace and inflation—the super boom.

CHAPTER

Yale Hirsch and the 500 Percent Move

If I have seen further, it is by standing upon the shoulders of giants.

—Sir Isaac Newton

In January 1977, my father, Yale Hirsch, founder of the Hirsch Organization, published a special report in his then newsletter, *Smart Money*. It was this special report—a prediction that the Dow would rise 500 percent over the next 13 years— that would later serve as the foundation of my Dow 38,820 super boom prediction.

Yale had published several articles over the previous three years proclaiming that the market had hit bottom during the fall of 1974. In 1974, with the Dow at 605, he printed a bold-faced headline of "BUY! BUY! BUY!" 18 times across the front page of *Smart Money*. After nearly two years of a debilitating bear market that drove the Dow down 45 percent, the S&P 500 48 percent, and Nasdaq 60 percent, Yale courageously went contrary to the crowd. Watergate, the OPEC oil embargo, and a devastating recession that began in November 1973 and would not end until March 1975 had destroyed consumer and investor confidence. But Yale sensed the tide had turned. The issue mailed a few days later on Friday, October 4, one day after both the S&P 500 and Nasdaq posted their lows for the remainder of the twentieth century.

In the January 1975 issue, published two days after the Dow's intraday low of 570 and three days after its closing low of 577.60, the two headlines on the front page of *Smart Money* read: "The Darkness Before the Dawn" and "Dow 800 by April 1975."

By April, the Dow had cleared 800 as Yale forecasted. Perhaps a bit too exuberantly, Yale then forecasted, "Dow 2,000 by 1980!" The Dow did not hit 2,000 until January 1987 for various reasons, one of which was the infamous double-dip recession of the early 1980s. Around the corner was Yale's 500 percent prediction, initially published one year later in April 1976. The January 1977 *Smart Money* Special Report was the culmination of many articles Yale wrote during 1976 as he researched super booms. It is a prescient forecast and the foundation of my own research into the trends—political, historical, and financial—that cause super booms. It is a glimpse into the history of the information super boom, the origins of the Hirsch Organization, and the discovery of the 500 percent equation. So I have reprinted sections of it here with my annotations and thoughts on similarities between 1976 and 2010. The full article is included as Appendix B at the end of the book. Appendix A includes Yale's portfolio recommendations from 1977 with my commentary and a quick review of each stock selection.

Smart Money—January 1977 Special Report

Invitation to a Super Boom

A SUPER BOOM rarely comes more than once in a generation. Unfortunately, it seems to follow a severely inflationary era which destroys stock values and leaves investors demoralized and disenchanted. Consequently, when the market begins its phoenix-like rise out of the ashes, the average investor, "scarred" and still remembering the pain of the past, fails to recognize the genuine buying opportunity of his lifetime. This report presents what I believe to be the most convincing evidence that a SUPER BOOM has already begun and is now in progress. Don't be late!

Yale Hirsch, Editor

Yale's opening paragraph could have begun the May 13, 2010, investor alert I sent to Almanac Investor subscribers detailing my Dow 38,820 super boom prediction.

Stocks Catch Up with Inflation Eventually

500% Moves After Both WW 1 & WW 2

Can It Happen Again? Dow 3420?

A number of acrophobes perspired a bit and donned parachutes when the Dow crossed 1,000 recently. If they are uneasy now, what will they do if the market climbs higher? And higher? And higher . . .?

Perhaps we can relieve some of their anxieties by putting Dow 1000 into perspective, considering the extent of inflation we have experienced in recent years and the fact that the market does catch up with inflation eventually. There have been three highly inflationary eras since the Civil War's 74 percent rate of inflation. These periods of high inflation were also war related—World War 1, World War 2 and Vietnam.

There's evidence that postwar super booms have existed for longer than previously thought. In mid-1862 the market bottomed. The Civil War had just begun. The New York Stock Exchange was not yet established at Broad and Wall and would not be until 1865.

Retroactive indices of stock prices show a long bull market running from 1862 to 1873 with stocks tripling over the 11-year span and suffering only one losing year in 1865 as the Civil War ended. In addition to the massive inflation from war spending, the first transcontinental telegraph and railroad as well as the abolishment of slavery served as catalysts to drive the long super boom.

World War 1

Prices slightly more than doubled in five years between 1915–1920. The Consumer Price Index (1967 = 100) climbed from approximately 30 to a dizzying 60. While the nation was suffering from two years of severe deflation and depression with stock market prices being slashed in half, the Dow began to rise out of the ashes. From 63.90 on August 24, 1921, it climbed to an intraday high of 386.10 on September 3, 1929, a spectacular **rise of 504 percent** for the 8-year period. Who could have dreamed it? This era likely gave birth to the adage, "Buy 'em and put 'em away."

Bear in mind that the Dow accomplished its feat despite many unfavorable conditions: the growth of communism and the beginning of fascism in Germany and Italy; monetary horrors such as the German "nightmare" inflation and the inability of our allies to pay their war debts; the Teapot Dome scandal; Prohibition and gangsterism; et al.

Through it all the Dow rolled on!

After World War 1, deflation brought the CPI down to the 50 level where it remained almost stationary throughout most of the twenties. The early thirties' deflation knocked the CPI down further to the 40 level, and there it stayed for the rest of the next decade. Interestingly, the rise in stock prices between the 1932 bottom and the 1937 top was quite respectable too—up 384 percent.

The buy and hold strategy is fine and well if you have a long-term time horizon and are buying relatively low and during long sideways secular bear markets. Warren Buffett, the ultimate buy and hold investor, is famous for saying, "Be fearful when others are greedy and greedy when others are fearful." In other words, buy when others are selling and sell when others are buying. That's contrarian investing. It's also an endorsement of market timing.

Sensible timing and trading strategies should be employed to preserve capital for infrequent buying opportunities. The post-March 2009 bull market rally is poised to move to new recovery highs in 2011, but as we approach the old October 2007 highs in the Dow 12,000–14,000 range in the middle of 2011, using some simple technical and fundamental indicators to reduce long equity exposure may become prudent. Timing was well rewarded during the several cyclical bull and bear markets that transpired from 1932 to 1942 as markets rallied and retreated and rallied again.

World War 2

The onset of the war brought about rising prices as usual. This resulted in a 74 percent rise in the cost of living between 1941–1948. The CPI rose from approximately 42 to 73.

After spending three years in the doldrums, the market began a long 16½-year rise on June 14, 1949, at Dow 160.62 (intraday). By January 18, 1966, when the Dow hit 1000.50 (intraday), investors once again had experienced a 500 percent climb following a super inflationary period. To be precise, **the rise measured 523 percent.** It should be noted that a small inflationary rate (averaging 1¾ percent a year) accompanied the market rise, bringing the CPI up to the 95 level.

Once again, we must point out that the Dow moved up despite many unsettling events along the way: the Korean War; the French defeat and withdrawal from Vietnam; McCarthyism; revolts in Poland, Hungary, Argentina; the Egyptian seizure of the Suez Canal and war with Israel, France and Britain; the Black Liberation movement; the Cuban missile crisis, the Kennedy assassination, etc.

According to the Bureau of Labor Statistics, the reported annual inflation rate as of October 2010 as measured by the CPI, which has gone through several notoriously inflation-masking revisions since the late 1970s (see Chapter 9), is 1.2 percent. Despite the recent deflationary environment and the first annual decline (–0.4 percent in 2009) since 1955, the CPI is up 30 percent since 1999, has averaged 2.5 percent during the 10-year period from 2000 to 2009, and is on pace to be 1.5 percent for 2010.

Vietnam War

The last decade has brought back a crunching inflation, unseen for a generation. War as usual was primarily responsible. Vietnam helped drive the CPI up from 95 to last year's 166, an increase of 75 percent.

Now, the market is "up at bat" again for the third time in a century following a war-induced, extraordinary inflation. On the two previous occasions, we witnessed smashing moves of over 500 percent. A similar move this time from the fall 1974 bottom of Dow 570 would bring us—fasten your seat-belts—up to **Dow 3420!**

Before anyone calls us crackpots or superbulls, let's calmly examine some numerical relationships as we attempt to put the 3420 figure into some perspective:

1. We first reached Dow 1000 in early 1966. When we recently, ten years later, hit this level again, it was **not** the same Dow 1000. The Consumer Price Index during the period rose from 95.4 percent to 166.7—an inflation of 74.7 percent—reducing the purchasing power of the dollar to 57.2 cents. Dow 1000 **now** is really worth only **Dow 572**. To equal 1966's Dow 1000, we should be at the **Dow 1747** level.
2. Earnings on the 30 Dow stocks in 1966 totaled $57.68. This year's earnings should reach $100. We estimate $115 Dow earnings in 1977, twice the earnings of 1966. If earnings are valued in **1977** as they were valued in **1966**, the Dow would have to be **2000**.
3. In our May 1975 issue, we explored the case for "Dow 2000 by 1980." Using accepted economic forecasting methods, we projected a Gross

National Product of $2.3 trillion (GNP in 1974 was $1.4 trillion). As stock prices and GNP tend to travel along the same general "flight path" (despite occasional divergences), we were able to graphically demonstrate that the two would cross paths in 1980 at Dow 2000.

4. We also (last year) estimated earnings of $150 for the Dow in 1980—which are not unreasonable. Price earnings ratios over the past 24 years at annual lows and highs have averaged 13–16. On this basis, the Dow could range between 1950–2400. If we take the *Value Line Survey* estimate of $170 earnings for the Dow in 1980, the average could range between 2210–2720.

5. Assuming an annual 4–5 percent rate of inflation, the CPI should cross 200 sometime in 1980. As the CPI was 95.4 when the Dow first touched the 1000 level in 1966, we would have to see the Dow over 2000 in 1980 just to keep up with inflation. If we take the $170 earnings estimate, which is almost triple the $57.68 earnings of 1966 when the Dow hit 1000, and multiply by the P/E ratio we enjoyed in 1966 we reach Dow 3000.

The last 500 percent move took 16½ years to achieve. If the next one takes the same length of time and began in the fall of 1974, then we have until 1990 to make it **three in a row.**

We are aware that the economy is more mature than in the past and that we can expect revolts, revolutions, environmental problems, monetary crises, scandals, droughts, more inflation, a few recessions and bear markets, not to mention a "plague" or two along the way. However, during the two previous 500 percent moves—or for that matter, the last 5,000 or more years—people always were afraid of something or other in the future. Somehow, we do seem to survive and overcome adversity.

From the chart showing the Dow and the Consumer Price Index plotted together (see Figure 5.1), we first observed the correlation between war, inflation and the subsequent catch-up by the market.

We further noticed the rectangular consolidation areas of approximately 18 years in length and having the same percentage range. These give the appearance of "launching pads" for the giant moves.

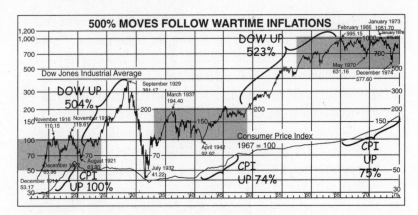

FIGURE 5.1 Yale's Original 500 Percent Move

The inflation/catch-up correlation is clear. World War I inflation (up 100%) followed by the 504% rise in stock prices during the twenties. Then we see the inflation of World War II (up 74%) and the subsequent long rise of the Dow of 523%. Finally, the Vietnam inflation of 75% (and not over yet) appears and the market begins its next(?) 500% rise from Dow 570 (intraday) in fall 1974 to ... Dow 3420?

Admittedly, things are different now. They always are. History never repeats exactly. The 1982–2000 super boom was different from the post-WWII suburban sprawl and TV boom, which was different from the Roaring '20s auto boom and all the other booms before.

The productivity gains of the information age and the 2007–2009 financial crisis have kept inflation more at bay during this bust period, not to mention the revisions to the CPI that mask inflation nowadays. We may be earlier in the inflation stage than when Yale made his forecast in 1976, but we contend that real inflation, the kind we all see and feel in our everyday purchases, is on the rise.

Many similarities between the mid-1970s and the present exist. Parallels between the Obama and Carter administrations have already been made by political pundits of all stripes and colors:

- Both are liberal Democrats who came into office with a sweeping victory on the heels of disappointment in the previous conservative Republican president (Carter followed Nixon and Obama followed Bush).
- Both inherited struggling economies and high unemployment.
- Vietnam was officially over in 1976, but Carter was still dealing with the political aftermath. In 2009, Obama became responsible for two wars he had originally opposed.
- As in the mid-1970s, we are currently suffering from the fallout of busted speculative bubbles and financial crises that have created a discouraged public and investment community.

The major difference between now and 1976 is that the headline inflation that caused so much pain during Carter's administration is at bay, for now.

Though inflation is relatively, or officially, in check at the moment, we are experiencing even more government spending than was seen in the 1970s. The spending on the wars in Iraq and Afghanistan and the global war on terror since 9/11 is staggering, estimated at $1.121 trillion[1] so far by the Congressional Research Service. Nobel Prize–winning economist Joseph Stiglitz estimates the total economic cost of the Iraq war alone to be $3 trillion.

Spending on the bailouts, fiscal stimulus, and quantitative easing is close to $4 trillion and growing. This will eventually result in significant inflation. Not to mention the extension of the Bush tax cuts, unemployment insurance benefits, and

---

[1] http://www.fas.org/sgp/crs/natsec/RL33110.pdf.

Social Security tax holiday, which could add another trillion. Our national debt has already swelled to $8 trillion since September 2001.

Even if inflation is muted by Fed policy, a boom will follow. We may not have the baby boomers or the incredibly liberating innovation of the microprocessor, which permeates nearly every aspect of current human existence, but a boom is brewing. There was no baby boom after WWI or WWII, but there were 500 percent stock market moves. Tremendous population growth during the Gilded Age did not result in a 1,447 percent market move as in 1982–2000. The information revolution was a rare perfect storm. Baby boomer consumer spending, the advent of the microprocessor, peace, and a supportive political environment all conspired to create the greatest stock market boom in history.

Though the next super boom may not be as tremendous as the boom of the 1980s and 1990s, a 500 percent move from the March 2009 lows is in the cards over the next 15 years. I expect inflation to catch up with government spending and for the stock market to catch up with inflation as it always has. I'll show you why and how in Part IV.

U.S. Entering One of the Most Prosperous Periods in Its History

Today most of the public and the pundits alike are worried. Some foresee a new surge of wild inflation followed by a crash. Others think the recovery is giving way to stagnation or a new slump. The one thing that hardly anyone expects is a long, healthy period of prosperity without serious recession or inflationary excesses. Therefore the theory of contrary opinion tells us that this is just what to look for.

The very factors that are being viewed with alarm are building the base for such a prosperous era. The slowdown in the recovery is allowing banks and business to **build up liquidity** needed for healthy future growth. Low levels of capital spending and building are creating

pent-up demand which is certain to stimulate the economy in the future. The widespread **skepticism and uncertainty is itself healthy**—just the opposite of universal enthusiasm and optimism during a dangerous runaway boom.

But what about unemployment, which is high and has increased lately? Isn't this a sign of trouble? No, it is just the opposite. Actually, **total employment has increased briskly** since the recession bottomed out last year. But the labor force has been growing at a tremendous rate due to a large influx of young people and married women, so business has not yet been able to absorb all the new job seekers.

A huge increase in our labor force is good. It means more production, larger capital investment, more goods and higher living standards. It also means growth in business and hence more earnings. This is particularly true since an increasing labor force allows employers to be more selective and hence favors greater productivity. These simple truths tend to be overlooked these days because of the annoying but temporary unemployment problem which attracts so much attention.

A large increase in total production will also serve to check inflation. Since inflation results from there being more money around than goods to buy, increasing the supply of goods to match money is a very effective way of halting it. When goods are scarce it's easy for suppliers to raise prices. When goods are abundant, competition to sell forces prices down.

Another factor contributing to productivity is technology, particularly the rapid introduction of new microcomputers based on single-chip circuits. These are being introduced into automobiles, appliances and above all into factory control systems, with tremendous improvements in efficiency. The results over the next decade will be a second industrial revolution.

Finally, there is the shift in general psychology away from the extremism and anger of a few years ago toward a more moderate, pragmatic attitude.

It has been in just such periods in the past that the stock market has made its most prolonged and biggest advances. And as *BusinessWeek* noted in January, at the start of the final quarter of the 20th century, the last 25 years of a century have been historically periods of great economic activity.

How right Yale was about the second industrial revolution, now known as the information revolution. "Microcomputers based on single-chip circuits" or microprocessors permeate everything in our lives. Few items in our homes and lives are without them. This is what enabled the PC, the Internet, the cell phone, wireless communications, and practically every major advancement since the 1970s.

But Yale was bit overoptimistic. We did suffer from wild inflation, crashes, and economic slumps over the next several years that gave voice to the term *stagflation,* a word thought to be coined in 1965 by British Conservative party finance minister Iain Macleod. But in his *Smart Money* advisory letter he navigated those shorter term gyrations while still insisting the big boom was coming. More price inflation = more market gains in the next boom.

We are suffering from similar unemployment woes now. We may avoid the painful stagflation of the 1970s, but public and political market sentiment is still negative. Over the next several years I expect continued discontent, political bickering, flash crashes, bear markets, inflation, and recession just like what was seen in the late '70s and early '80s.

Despite all this volatility, the market bottom and top will hold while the government and the public figure out better policies that stimulate lasting economic expansion. When the economy has healed, the next enabling technology combined with a wave of consumer and business spending and inflation launches the next super boom.

Super Boom Ahead?

Happy Birthday, America!

One of the most useful indicators predicting future business conditions is the **Debit/Loan ratio**, monitored by Bank Credit Analyst of Montreal. This is the ratio of bank debits to business loans at the banks. Bank debits are simply check clearings, a measure of the rate at which money is turning over and hence a measure of business activity.

The logic of this indicator is that if business is expanding much faster than debt is increasing, the situation is healthy. If on the other hand large increases in debt are needed to support slow gains in business activity, you have a weak, dangerous situation. The record shows that this debit/loan ratio has been excellent in predicting business profits.

During the last thirty years, this indicator has reached peaks as high as +8 to +12, usually in "boom buildup" periods such as 1954, 1961 and 1971. The latest reading, however, has run off the scale at **+18** (see Figure 5.2). You have to go back to the giant wartime (World War II) business expansion to find anything comparable.

While the debit/loan ratio has only a fair record as a stock market indicator, it may be telling us something very important about stocks as of now. With the price/earnings ratio of the Dow recently under 12 (and many secondary stocks much cheaper), the market should certainly go higher unless the business recovery starts to falter. But the debit/loan ratio says that, on the contrary, business earnings will go much higher. The conclusion as to the stock market seems obvious. Prices should go to much higher levels despite normal reactions and consolidations from time to time.

The accompanying chart of the Bank Credit Analyst's Debit-Loan Ratio (see Figure 5.2) portrays an extremely bullish picture. This ratio is high (and bullish) when business is expanding without a significant increase in borrowing and low (and bearish) when business is flat or declining in face of rapid expansion in borrowing. This confirms other data, all of which points toward greater business liquidity. The recession scared businessmen into cleaning up their balance sheets instead of planning for endless growth on borrowed money.

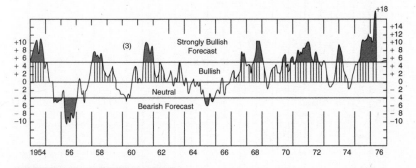

FIGURE 5.2   Debit-Loan Ratio
Source: Yale Hirsch, Jeffrey Hirsch and The Hirsch Organization Inc. 1977.

It is precisely such a sound financial base that has been needed to launch a sustained era of high prosperity. In the last decade, as soon as the economy warmed up, it became subject to strains from tight money and excessive debt. This time it should be different, and that is what so many perpetual pessimists have not yet recognized.

More Evidence of a Boom in the Making

An excessive spurt in business loans usually spells trouble ahead for the economy. It means that businesses are taking on heavy risks. They may be doing this through necessity, to finance slow moving inventory, or through over-optimism leading to a big expansion in plant capacity. In either case they will be vulnerable to any economic slowdown. The sharp rise in debt in 1973–1974 contributed greatly to the severity of that recession.

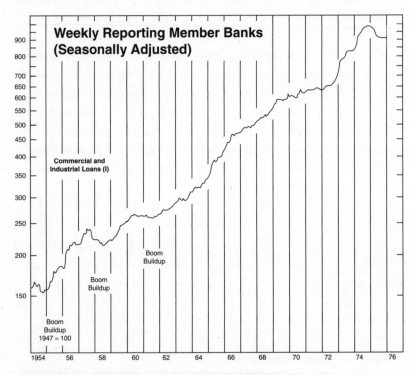

FIGURE 5.3   Commercial and Industrial Loans
Source: Yale Hirsch, Jeffrey Hirsch and The Hirsch Organization Inc. 1977.

On the other hand a sharp reduction in debt places businesses on a sounder footing. With the burden of interest charges and debt repayment behind them, companies are financially healthier and the stage is set for expansion. A look at the chart (see Figure 5.3) shows that business has been moving into such a strong position over the last 18 months.

Business bank loans have decreased more than at any time in over twenty years, both in absolute terms and percentagewise.

In the '70s, when consumers were still using paper checks, the debit-loan ratio was a useful measure of transaction volume at banks. A high ratio implied favorable business activity that was not being supported by increases in debt.

Bank debits are not tracked in the same manner as they were in 1976. In fact, the Fed stopped publishing the bank debits report that year. The velocity of money is used nowadays. It measures turnover in the money supply, or business activity. While the velocity of M1 in Figure 5.4 has been flatlining since the end of the recession in June 2009 after its steep 2008–2009 decline, the velocity of the larger measures of money supply, M2 in Figure 5.5 and MZM in Figure 5.6, have

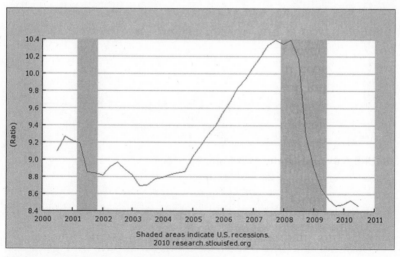

FIGURE 5.4   Velocity of M1 Money Stock
Source: Federal Reserve Bank of St. Louis.

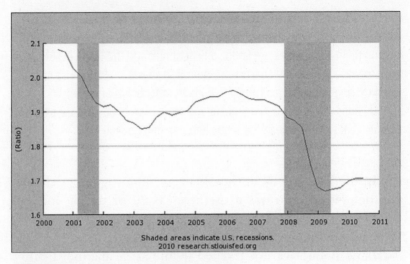

FIGURE 5.5   Velocity of M2 Money Stock
Source: Federal Reserve Bank of St. Louis.

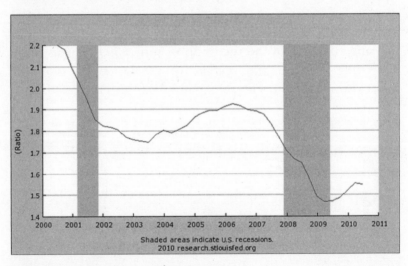

FIGURE 5.6   Velocity of MZM Money Stock
Source: Federal Reserve Bank of St. Louis.

been upticking since the end of the recession and have only leveled off the past two quarters.

Commercial and industrial loans as shown in Figure 5.7 have fallen precipitously since late 2008. A sustained rise in the velocity of money over the next several years without a

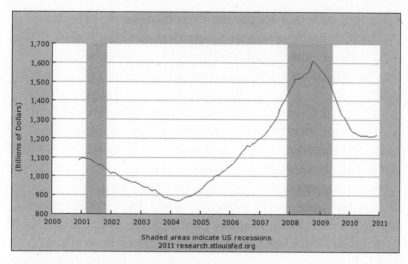

FIGURE 5.7   Commercial and Industrial Loans
Source: Board of Governors of the Federal Reserve System.

corresponding rise in commercial and industrial loans will herald the beginning of the next boom. Business activity will be increasing as businesses begin to put the record amounts of cash they currently have on their balance sheets back to work.

Is Massive Rise in Earnings Being Overlooked by Investors?

Corporate earnings have been soaring at a rate which could soon carry them to 1974 levels. What's more, these earnings are for real—they cannot be attributed to phony inventory write-ups. There is every reason to expect them to go much higher since the recovery is still in an early stage.

The stage for a healthy recovery has been set by the 1973–1974 recession which forced businessmen to reduce inventories, drop unprofitable lines, increase efficiency and build up liquidity. This spells good profits now when business is still recovering and could mean unbelievable gains by the time a real boom develops. **YET** skepticism still prevails among many money managers and especially the investing public. **WHY?**

The answer lies in investor psychology, where extremes in optimism and pessimism are not easily overcome even though a market has turned.

At market bottoms disenchantment with common stocks is so great and investment prospects so bleak that only a handful of courageous or contrary thinking investors are able to exploit bargain prices. Likewise, at market tops, the outlook for the stock market and economy is so convincingly positive that again, only a few are able to see beyond the current euphoria when "business could not be better" and "get out at the top." The process of developing confidence following bear-market bottoms and tempering blind optimism after market tops, is a gradual one. As a result, a correlation of fundamentals (earnings) to stock prices is often irregular.

For example (see Figure 5.8), during the past fifteen years the market has fluctuated widely but has really only "netted out a gain of 40 percent or 2½ percent annually (dotted line B'-C'). That's a far cry from the previous 13 years (1948–1961) when the average racked up a 375 percent gains (A'-B').

The trend of corporate profits during these two periods, however, was reversed with a gain of 280 percent during 1961–1975 (B-C) and a mere 30 percent gain in 1948–1961 (A-B) when the market was its strongest. Such a lack of correlation of stock prices and earnings between the two

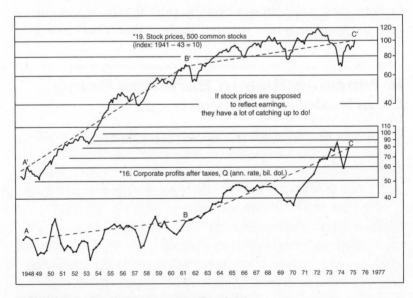

FIGURE 5.8 Stock Prices versus Earnings
Source: Yale Hirsch, Jeffrey Hirsch and The Hirsch Organization Inc. 1977.

periods is mainly attributable to psychological factors. Immediately after World War II, corporate earnings soared but the general opinion was that these earnings were just a fluke, that they would collapse as soon as post-war demand was satisfied and a new depression set in. The market advance of 1948–1961 reflected the gradual development of confidence and belief these earnings levels were real and could even grow. Eventually, by 1961, confidence had given way to over-optimism and many stocks sold at unrealistic prices.

It was only natural then, that for some years after 1961 the market failed to keep up with rising earnings. Even though stocks advanced, they were gradually adjusting to more normal price/earnings ratios.

Price earnings ratios are not as attractive at the end of 2010 as they were at the time of Yale's prediction. But they are not astronomical either. At the end of 1976 P/E ratios on the Dow and S&P 500 were around 10. Currently, the Dow sports a P/E of 14.5 and the S&P 500's is about 17. Profits jumped in 2010 and continue to rise. A good deal of that has come from cost-cutting. In order for real growth to take shape, we will need a pickup in top-line revenue growth. The stage is set for revenue growth over the next several years. Costs and margins have been cut to the bone, so when revenue growth picks up more will fall to the bottom line.

A Portfolio for the Super Boom

How can you benefit most effectively from the super boom which we project for the years ahead? No question but that a good portfolio of stocks should do fabulously well in such a period—but which stocks?

...This core portfolio is recommended as a long-term commitment for the major part of your investment capital. It would then be held in good markets or bad, regardless of favorable or unfavorable news, for full participation in the big trend. A smaller part of your funds may be reserved for more active management, moving in and out of the market in more volatile stocks, etc. You will feel more secure and more able to trade effectively if you know that you have this solid base of excellent investments providing a substantial, growing field.

By holding such a diversified, high-quality portfolio patiently, we believe you will do far better than the great majority of in-and-out traders who are so busy chasing passing fluctuations that they completely miss the major trend.

Yale's 1977 stock picks can be found in Appendix B of the book, with my annotations and a statistical review of each selection. They are an interesting glimpse into the market over thirty years ago.

The last chapter of this book contains portfolio strategies and specific recommendations for the next fifteen years. This includes recommendations for the five- to ten-year sideways market as well as investments appropriate for the following super boom. The next super boom will begin around 2017 and run to at least 2025, carrying the Dow to at least 38,820.

A Perfect Long-Term Inflation Hedge?

Why the Stock Market of Course!

Yes! Not once in this century has the market failed to conquer inflation over **any** 25-year period. [As shown in Figure 5.9,] a $1,000 investment in the Dow Jones industrials for all the 23 periods below **with dividends reinvested annually**, less any taxes and all buying commissions, would have resulted in a "Total Dow Return" of $11,563 on average. Meanwhile, $1,000 deposited in a typical savings account and earning the prevailing interest rate, compounded annually less taxes, would have grown to only $1,712.

Adjusting for each period's inflation reduces the "total Dow return" to $5,648 and the savings account's to $853. Only in three of the 23 periods did a typical saver manage to hold onto his original $1,000 worth of purchasing power. Next time a friend gripes about "the market," send him a copy of this page!

			Adjusted For Inflation		
25-Year Periods	**Total Dow Return** *	**Regular Savings Account** **	**Total Dow Return**	**Regular Savings Account**	**$1,000 Actual Cash**

What $1,000 Grew to During 25-Year Periods

25-Year Periods	Total Dow Return *	Regular Savings Account **	Total Dow Return	Regular Savings Account	$1,000 Actual Cash
1928–1953	$2,472	$1,580	$1,575	$1,006	$637
1929–1954	4,272	1,556	2,687	978	629
1930–1955	7,590	1,536	4,744	960	625
1931–1956	15,696	1,524	8,918	865	568
1932–1957	17,451	1,519	8,513	740	488
1933–1958	13,998	1,522	6,273	682	448
1934–1959	15,593	1,527	7,153	700	459
1935–1960	10,227	1,539	4,713	709	461
1936–1961	9,669	1,559	4,518	728	467
1937–1962	12,500	1,583	5,896	746	472
1938–1963	11,408	1,607	5,209	737	457
1939–1964	13,415	1,634	6,070	739	452
1940–1965	16,472	1,662	7,408	735	442
1941–1966	15,719	1,700	7,145	772	455
1942–1967	16,582	1,739	8,128	852	490
1943–1968	15,047	1,778	7,524	889	500
1944–1969	11,379	1,819	5,471	874	481
1945–1970	9,438	1,867	4,390	868	465
1946–1971	10,842	1,917	5,289	935	488
1947–1972	11,983	1,968	6,408	1,052	535
1948–1973	10,043	2,024	5,429	1,094	541
1949–1974	6,432	2,078	3,092	999	481
1950–1975	7,448	2,129	3,340	954	448
Averages	**$11,563**	**$1,712**	**$5,648**	**$853**	**$500**

* Dividends reinvested annually less 23% income tax and 2% commissions on all purchases. (Capital gains taxes and selling commissions not deducted.)

** Actual N.Y. savings bank accounts with interest compounded annually after 23% income tax.

FIGURE 5.9 $1,000 Grew Table

Stocks are still the best hedge against long term inflation. In Part IV is a new comparison of stocks versus gold—the supposed de facto inflation hedge of all time.

In June 1980, Yale held his first *Smart Money* seminar at the Tarrytown Hilton, right over the Hudson River from our current offices in Nyack, New York, under the theme: "Getting Ready For The First Bull Market Of The Eighties." The first bull market of the 1980s had begun on March 27, 1980, for the S&P 500 and NASDAQ, and on April 21, 1980, for the Dow.

FIGURE 5.10   DOW 3420! T-Shirt

The four-day soiree was headlined by keynote speaker Louis Rukeyser. Despite four years of rough sledding, Yale had navy blue t-shirts made up with white lettering that read "DOW 3420!" (see Figure 5.10) as giveaways to seminar attendees. One box was saved for posterity.

PART III

BOOMS AND BUSTS OF THE TWENTIETH CENTURY

Human history is replete with episodes of economic booms and busts. Tremendous advancements in technology have not shielded modern civilization from volatility. Throughout our amazing history, war and financial panics have been a central force in the advancement of humanity.

Massive inflation brought on by the American Civil War contributed to the Reconstruction-era boom from 1863 to 1873 as the transcontinental railroad, completed in 1869, connected America from coast to coast. The financial panic of 1873 kicked off a worldwide economic depression that lasted into 1896, known in the United States as the Long Depression. The National Bureau of Economic Research lists the contraction from October 1873 to March 1879 at 65 months, the longest in their records, eclipsing the 43-month contraction of the Great Depression. Much like the depression of 1873, rampant speculation, railroad overbuilding, and dubious financial practices ushered in another depression in 1893 that caused double-digit unemployment for the next five to six years.

As the nineteenth century wound to a close, the advent of the telegraph, railroads, telephones, internal combustion engines, automobiles, ocean liners, electric light bulbs, and radio laid the groundwork for what Stephen Moore and Julian L. Simon of the Cato Institute called "The Greatest Century That Ever Was." War and peace, manias and slumps, inflation and innovation have always impacted economics, wealth, and the global markets. But when the Dow Jones Industrial Average was published for the first time on May 26, 1896—also, coincidentally, my birthday—the world had for the first time a consistent, trackable index that could objectively measure the fluctuations of prosperity and the prospects for growth.

The most quintessential financial market gauge ever devised, the Dow Jones Industrial Average benchmark, continued to mature over the next several decades in conjunction with the creation of the Federal Reserve System in 1913. In the words of turn-of-the-century humorist and showman Will Rogers, "There have been three great inventions since the beginning of time: the fire, the wheel, and central banking."

CHAPTER

Panics, World War I, and the Roaring Twenties

*We step upon the threshold of 1900, which leads to the new
century, facing a still brighter dawn for human civilization.*
—*New York Times* editorial, December 31, 1899

The markets were on a wild ride at the start of the twentieth century. Global volatility would moderate considerably during this century as the international playing field leveled off, but the early years were trying. The new century began under the unfortunate auspices of a bear market: From April 1899 to September 1900, the Dow lost 31.5 percent as immigrants fleeing oppression and turmoil in Europe flooded America at the rate of 100 per hour.

A brief nine-month bull market that lifted the Dow 48 percent ended with the beginning of the battle to control the railroads, which caused a run on stocks and a market crash known as the Panic of 1901. The assassination of President McKinley only exacerbated the dire markets. Newly elected President Teddy Roosevelt successfully restored stability to the market in 1902 when he enforced the 1890 Sherman Antitrust Act and busted up the constituents that were manipulating and controlling markets.

Stability did not last. With residual effects from the 1898 Spanish-American War forcing U.S. troops to be sent to Panama (in 1902), Honduras, and Santo Domingo, souring the mood of the country, the Rich Man's Panic of 1903 struck, caused by high interest rates, excessive stock issuance, the continuing battle for control of the Northern Pacific Railroad, and Roosevelt's attacks on the trusts. It was followed by a two-year recession that drove the Dow down 46 percent to its historical low for the century on November 9, 1903.

Then, at the depths of the recession, bulls ruled Wall Street from November 1903 to January 1906 as the Dow gained 144 percent. Leaps in industrial production and manufacturing helped power the markets as Henry Ford founded Ford Motor in 1903. The internal combustion engine also powered the Wright Brothers' flight at Kitty Hawk, North Carolina, in December 1903. During this miniboom real estate values soared in New York and antitrust battles were waged. When Roosevelt began his antitrust suit against Standard Oil in 1906, which was finally broken up into 34 companies in 1911, the bull market began to falter. The 1906 San Francisco earthquake also weighed heavily on the economy.

Then the 1907 Bankers' Panic slashed the Dow nearly in half, a 48.5 percent drop from January 1906 to November 1907. Much like the Fed's maneuvers and government-engineered bailouts in 2008, the U.S. Treasury in 1907 bought bonds to offset the market decline, and at the very bottom J. P. Morgan orchestrated a cash infusion with other bankers to shore up stock prices. The Dow rallied 90 percent over the next two years, but stalled just below the 1906 high as a secular bear market arrived that would keep the Dow range-bound between 50[1] and 120 until 1925.

Double-dip two-year recessions, from January 1910 to January 1912 and January 1913 to December 1914, squashed

---

[1]Adjusted for the new 1916 Dow.

the economy and market as the federal government continued to rein in powerful corporate trusts. Henry Ford's moving assembly line in 1913 would enable mass production of automobiles and help power the super boom of the Roaring Twenties. The onset of World War I closed the New York Stock Exchange for four months from July to December 1914, putting a floor under the market until the Great Depression.

The First Components: World War I

A super boom requires three components. The first is a period of peace following large-scale global military combat. After two years of war in the Balkans, it was the assassination of Austrian Archduke Franz Ferdinand by a Serb on June 28, 1914, that sparked World War I. On July 28, 1914, after a period of failed diplomatic efforts, Austria-Hungary declared war and invaded Serbia. A vast array of alliances and ambitions set off a domino effect as conflicts erupted across Europe and then the world.

The New York Stock Exchange closed from July 31, 1914 until December 12, 1914 (see Figure 6.1, points 1 and 2). Much of the escalation of the war occurred during this time. When the NYSE reopened, a bull market began as the United States maintained its neutrality in WWI and supported the Allied war effort over the next two years. Germany's bombing of the United Kingdom on January 19, 1915 (Figure 6.1, point 3), and sinking of a U.S. freighter on January 28 pushed the market down briefly. Stocks also took a dive when a German U-boat sank the British passenger ship *Lusitania*, killing 1,198 of the 1,959 on board (Figure 6.1, point 4), which turned international public opinion against Germany and began a process that would lead to U.S. entry in the war. Germany's bombing of Paris in January 1916 roiled the market for six months.

It was not until Wilson was elected to a second term in November 1916 (Figure 6.1, point 6) and Germany made peace overtures in December 1916 that stocks ended the first bull market since the reopening of the market that had pushed the Dow up

World War I begins Austria-Hungary invades Serbia 7/28/1914
1 7/30/1914 NYSE Closes due to WWI
2 12/12/1914 New York Stock Exchange re-opens
3 1/19/1915 UK is bombed by Germany
4 5/7/1915 Lusitania is sunk by a German U-boat killing 1,198
5 1/29/1916 Paris is bombed by Germany
6 11/4/1916 Wilson defeats Hughes US presidential election
7   1/31/1917 U-boats engage in unrestricted submarine warfare
8   2/3/1917 US breaks off diplomatic relations with Germany
9   4/6/1917 US declares war on Germany
10 6/5/1917 Conscription begins in the United States
11 12/26/1917 Wilson takes control of nearly all railroads
World War I ends Armistice signed with Germany 11/11/1918

FIGURE 6.1   Dow Jones Performance during WWI

110.5 percent to a new all-time high of 110.15 on November 21, 1916. One of the 10 worst bear markets since 1900 ensued that knocked the Dow down 40 percent over the next 13 months as the war turned uglier. Germany began attacking neutral ships in the war zone and engaged in unrestricted submarine warfare in January 1917. Diplomatic relations with Germany were broken off in February, and the United States declared war on April 6, 1917.

Conscription in the United States began in June 1917, and when President Wilson took control of nearly all the railroads the day after Christmas 1917 (Figure 6.1, point 11), the low of the bear market was secured. The Dow rallied over 81 percent for nearly two years as Allied victories forced an end to the war. An armistice was signed on Sunday, November 11, 1918, which is now celebrated as Veterans Day. But the 1920s super boom would not commence until the final peace accord was signed between the United States and Germany in August 1921.

Roaring Twenties

The second component in the super boom equation is dramatic inflation. Driven by a 2,500 percent increase in government

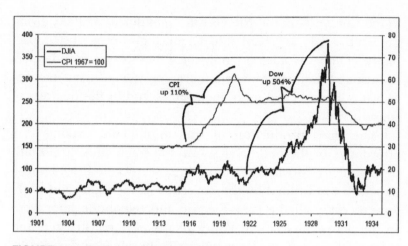

FIGURE 6.2   DJIA and CPI, 1901–1934
Sources: Stock Trader's Almanac; www.bls.gov.

spending from when the United States entered World War I in 1917 until 1919, consumer prices more than doubled with the Consumer Price Index rising 110 percent from 1915 to 1920. Inflation finally settled down in the 1920s, which left room for the economy and the stock market to catch up. Figure 6.2 illustrates this meteoric rise in inflation and the subsequent and corresponding boom in the Dow.

As President Harding promised on the campaign trail, "normalcy" returned to politics. Peacetime, inflation, political cooperation, and systemic changes in social and cultural behavior provided the base, but it was the third and final component, an array of enabling technologies, that completed the super boom equation. The internal combustion engine, the automobile, the discovery of powered flight, and the assembly-line method of production fueled a dynamic nine years of artistic creativity, liberalization of social mores, and financial speculation, which carried the Dow up 504 percent from 1921 to 1929.

Prohibition's ban on alcohol did little to quell its demand and usage. In fact, it created a taboo factor that fueled organized crime and speculative fervor. But it was the next amendment to the Constitution, the Nineteenth Amendment in 1920, giving women the right to vote, that had a much greater positive impact on the country. Women not only voted, but this newfound equality inspired women to work more, providing many families with two incomes and more money to spend in the new age of consumerism.

The mass production of the automobile, making cars affordable for the middle class, was the single most important development. Movies and radio also skyrocketed. New infrastructure was funded by the government for roads and highways to carry all the cars. Electric and telephone lines were strung across the nation. Power plants were constructed and cities of all sizes grew as new industries, business, and construction sprung up from coast to coast.

All this expansion and innovation created an air of invincibility that fanned the flames of rampant speculation and irresponsible financial activity. For six consecutive years, from October 1923 to September 1929, the Dow marched steadily higher, despite two relatively mild recessions in 1923–1924 and 1927–1928. At the height of the final six-year bull market with the Dow up 344.5 percent—still more than the 294.8 percent in 1990–1998—individual investors could buy stocks on 90 percent margin.

It all came crashing down on October 28 and 29, 1929, with a run on stocks that caused the worst crash in the history of the New York Stock Exchange. The Dow fell 23 percent in two days and 47.9 percent in 71 days. All booms come to an end, but never before or since with such a precipitous decline.

CHAPTER

Depression, World War II, and the Baby Boom

These are days when many are discouraged. In the 93 years of my life, depressions have come and gone. Prosperity has always returned and will again.
— John D. Rockefeller, July 8, 1932

At 71 days, the great crash of 1929 would hold the record for the shortest bear market for 58 years until the crash of October 1987 nearly matched the two-day affair in 1929 with a one-day 22.6 percent plunge. But Black Monday, as the 1987 crash is known, was a mere blip in the super boom of the 1980s and 1990s. The crash of 1929 was the first wave of an unprecedented decline.

Ethical abuses and financial shenanigans surfaced on Wall Street shortly thereafter and the crash gathered greater momentum. The loss of $25 billion of wealth in one day after a decade of expansion shattered investor confidence for years.

The decline in stock prices was so swift and devastating that it disrupted commerce, causing bankruptcies, business closures, frozen credit, job losses, depressed consumer spending, bank failures, and severe deflation. On top of financial calamity came natural disaster. A major drought began consuming North American prairie lands from Canada to Texas in 1930, crushing agricultural prices. Coupled with poor farming practices, this drought turned into the Dust Bowl that destroyed 100 million acres from 1930 to 1936 in and around the panhandles of Texas and Oklahoma.

Stocks plunged like no other time in modern history, suffering huge double-digit losses four years straight and lasting through President Hoover's entire term. No other presidential term has had stock market losses in every year. By the July 8, 1932 low, the Dow had lost 89.2 percent of its value. Its 1929 level of 381.17 would not be seen again until November 1954, over 25 years later.

During the shortest bull market on record, the Dow spiked 93.9 percent in 61 days from July to September 1932. Then a five-and-a-half-month relapse brought the Dow back down 37.2 percent on February 27, 1933, just five days before Franklin D. Roosevelt was sworn in as president. By the time FDR began to implement stimulus programs and financial regulations in 1933, the damage was done and the country and the world had already plunged into the Great Depression.

One of FDR's first orders of business was a nine-day bank moratorium one day after taking office. By the end of March 1933, 12,800 of 18,000 banks had reopened. The United States went off the gold standard in April and passed the Glass-Steagall Act in June, which established the Federal Deposit Insurance Corporation (FDIC) and mandated the separation of commercial banks and investment banks.

Prohibition was repealed in December as the entire country needed a drink. U.S. unemployment reached a peak of 25 percent in 1933 at the depths of the Depression. The reforms continued in 1934 with the creation of the Securities and Exchange Commission and FDR's New Deal programs. A four-year expansion from 1933 to 1937 was only interrupted briefly by a mild five-and-a-half-month bear market in 1934 that clipped 22.8 percent off the Dow, the smallest bear market decline in 10 years.

But as America was rebuilding, totalitarianism was brewing in Europe and in Asia. Japan invaded China, the Soviet Union, and Mongolia. In the spring of 1937, a year-long bear market and recession gripped the United States. European war drums and Wall Street scandals scared investors, and FDR's attempts to balance the budget depressed the economy even further. From March 1937 to March 1938, the Dow fell 49.1 percent, its third worst bear market decline since the creation of the industrial average in 1896. In April 1938, FDR reversed course on balancing the budget and increased spending. This began an economic expansion that continued through World War II and finally ended the Great Depression.

World War II

Germany annexed Czechoslovakia in March 1939 and German tanks rolled into Poland on September 1, 1939, signifying the start of World War II. See Figure 7.1 for a detailed graphical look at the Dow during WWII. Germany and Italy aligned and Britain and France declared war on Germany. In 1940, Germany invaded Western Europe and France fell in June.

Meanwhile, Japan and China waged the Second Sino-Japanese War from October 1938 to December 1941 when Japan bombed Pearl Harbor and joined the Axis Powers while China sided with the Allies. By the end of 1941 the world was completely at war with the Axis Powers headed by Germany, Japan, and Italy. The Allies were led by the British, French, Soviets, Chinese, and United States.

The beginning of WWII caused a three-year losing run for stocks from 1939 to 1941. When the United States entered the war in 1942, the Dow put in a low of 92.99 on April 28. To this day, the Dow has never dipped below that April low. The fourth longest bull market ever would rally the Dow 128.7 percent over

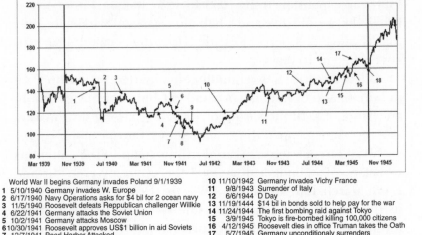

World War II begins Germany invades Poland 9/1/1939
1 5/10/1940 Germany invades W. Europe
2 6/17/1940 Navy Operations asks for $4 bil for 2 ocean navy
3 11/5/1940 Roosevelt defeats Reppublican challenger Willkie
4 6/22/1941 Germany attacks the Soviet Union
5 10/2/1941 Germany attacks Moscow
6 10/30/1941 Roosevelt approves US$1 billion in aid Soviets
7 12/7/1941 Pearl Harbor Attacked
8 1/26/1942 US forces arrive in Europe I
9 2/27/1942 US$ Langley is sunk by Japanese warplanes
10 11/10/1942 Germany invades Vichy France
11 9/8/1943 Surrender of Italy
12 6/6/1944 D Day
13 11/19/1444 $14 bil in bonds sold to help pay for the war
14 11/24/1944 The first bombing raid against Tokyo
15 3/9/1945 Tokyo is fire-bombed killing 100,000 citizens
16 4/12/1945 Roosevelt dies in office Truman takes the Oath
17 5/7/1945 Germany unconditionaly surrenders
18 8/6/1945 "Little Boy" & "Fat Man" dropped on Japan
World War II ends V-J Day Imperial Japan surrenders 8/15/1945

FIGURE 7.1   Dow Jones during World War II

the next four years as Allied victories raised spirits and the war machine stimulated the economy. WWII ended on September 2, 1945, when the Japanese surrendered to the United States.

The onset of the war brought rising prices as usual. This resulted in a 74 percent rise in the cost of living between 1941 and 1948. The CPI rose from approximately 42 to 73. Stocks and the economy consolidated over the next three years from mid-1946 to mid-1949 when the next super boom began.

Why Not Korea?

The Korean War was a major international military entanglement that cost the United States over 36,500 lives. It lasted for three years, longer than the U.S. involvement in WWI, but it did not have much effect on the market. The Dow lost 12 percent over two and a half weeks from June 25, 1950, when North Korea invaded South Korea. See Figure 7.2 for a detailed graphical look at the Dow during the Korean War. Though this war pitted the new superpowers of the USA and USSR against each other in a preamble of the Vietnam

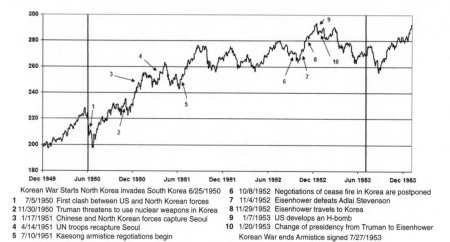

Korean War Starts North Korea invades South Korea 6/25/1950
1 7/5/1950 First clash between US and North Korean forces
2 11/30/1950 Truman threatens to use nuclear weapons in Korea
3 1/17/1951 Chinese and North Korean forces capture Seoul
4 4/14/1951 UN troops recapture Seoul
5 7/10/1951 Kaesong armistice regotiations begin

6 10/8/1952 Negotiations of cease fire in Korea are postponed
7 11/4/1952 Eisenhower defeats Adlai Stevenson
8 11/29/1952 Eisenhower travels to Korea
9 1/7/1953 US develops an H-bomb
10 1/20/1953 Change of presidency from Truman to Eisenhower
Korean War ends Armistice signed 7/27/1953

FIGURE 7.2   DJIA during Korean War, 1950–1953

conflict, the markets only took a brief hit before resuming an uptrend.

The Korean War did keep a lid on the post-WWII super boom as the Dow meandered sideways from 1951 to 1953. The recent victory and the brutal atomic bomb attack on Japan were fresh in the world's mind, muting the impact of the Korean War on the market. U.S. forces from the Pacific theater of WWII were still in the vicinity so mobilization was less of an undertaking. Leftover WWII material was readily available, reducing military spending by the United States and the newly created NATO.

The Korean War did not consume the entire world or U.S. coffers. Inflation was nowhere in sight. The CPI retreated for a year and a half from late 1948 to early 1950 and only increased 13 percent during the war. While tragic, the Korean War was just a brief pause in the economic and financial boom of the 1950s and 1960s. No significant inflation, no super boom.

Consumer Boom

After a post-WWII bear market and recession from mid-1946 to mid-1947, the economy and stock market began to find their footing. The Marshall Plan rebuilt Europe from 1947 to 1951, but the cold war began as the Truman Doctrine combated Communism.

Nevertheless, by 1949 happy days were here again. The post-WWII consumer boom vaulted the economy and stock market higher for the next 16 years on a steady diet of enabling technologies and an expanding middle class. A society polarized by urban centers and farms embraced suburban sprawl during the baby boom as common appliances became readily available to the burgeoning middle class. Everyone needed a house filled with TVs, refrigerators, washers, dryers, and so forth. Roads were built so folks could commute to their jobs in the big city.

The year 1955 began the 26-year Democratic control of Congress, and the Montgomery bus boycott launched the civil rights movement. Soviet tanks entered Hungary in October 1956 to crush the rebellion, effectively capping the post–Korean War bull market. Cold war relations deteriorated as tensions grew between East and West. With the civil rights movement in full swing for two years, Congress passed the first civil rights bill in April 1957. Eisenhower was forced to use U.S. troops in September 1957 to quell the segregation crisis in Little Rock, Arkansas. The passage of the Civil Rights Act of 1957 and the related racial standoff in Arkansas exacerbated the nascent bear market into a waterfall decline that plunged the Dow down 18.8 percent from July to a bottom in October 1957, shaving 21.6 percent off the S&P 500 for the year.

Following the 1957 post–election year bottom, and all the negativity during the preceding two years, stocks went virtually straight up in midterm 1958 as the S&P gained 38.1 percent for all of 1958. By election day the S&P was already up 28.9 percent for the year and tacked on another 7.1 percent by year end. Such action has not occurred in a midterm year since.

Despite a 57 percent presidential approval rating just prior to the midterm elections, Ike's Republicans lost 48 House seats (23.9 percent), increasing the Democratic advantage 283 to

156 and setting the stage for a young John F. Kennedy to take back the White House for the Democrats in 1960.

Mutual fund buying grew to a frenzy in 1958 as margins were raised to 90 percent. Ike ended the steel strike in 1959 as Vice President Nixon toured the USSR and Krushchev visited the USA. Peace and prosperity pushed the S&P for a total bull market advance of 50.5 percent from October 1957 to January 1960. Cold war machinations spooked the market in 1960 when the USSR shot down a U.S. U-2 spy plane in Soviet territory in May, and Castro seized U.S. oil refineries in June–July, which led to the now 50-year-old Cuban embargo. A recession and a fierce presidential election battle between sitting Vice President Nixon and JFK bottomed stocks out just before the election in October 1960.

The Bay of Pigs fiasco in August 1961 put an end to the JFK honeymoon bull market. JFK's 1962 crackdown on the steel industry in April sent Wall Street reeling. Kennedy's stare down with the steel industry over price increases, the Cuban missile crisis, and stirrings in Vietnam with U.S. military personnel in 1962 created a double bottom in June and October. Kennedy's 61 percent approval rating ahead of the midterm elections helped his fellow Democrats keep control of the House, losing only four seats.

With the bottom already in place, the S&P was down only 12.7 percent for the year on election day, rallying 8.1 percent by year end. The S&P had lost 28.0 percent from the December 1961 post–election year high to the June midterm bear market low.

Martin Luther King, Jr. made his "I Have a Dream" speech on August 28, 1963, during the "March on Washington" at the National Mall, electrifying an estimated crowd of 200,000. From the June 1962 bear market low, the S&P rallied 77.9 percent over the next four years to the February 1966 top. See Figure 7.3 for a look at the DJIA and the CPI during this time period.

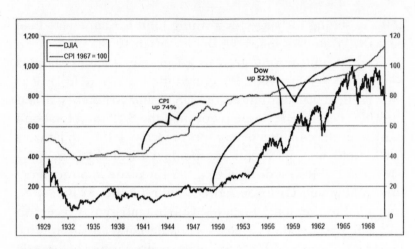

FIGURE 7.3   DJIA and CPI
Sources: Stock Trader's Almanac; www.bls.gov.

In November 1963 the South Vietnamese government was overthrown and President Kennedy was shot. By the summer of 1964 the Gulf of Tonkin Resolution was signed and the Vietnam War was officially under way. Also beginning was a secular bear market that would last 18 years.

Irrespective of the cold war, stocks kept rocking and rolling through the 1950s and 1960s. Truman, Eisenhower, JFK, and Martin Luther King, Jr. were visionary leaders that inspired the nation. Kennedy's agenda to put a man on the moon in less than a decade was successful when his successors supported and completed the project.

King forged an agenda of equal rights and justice for all people through nonviolent protest. Urbanization and mass production fueled corporate profits. And the Dow sailed 523 percent higher from 1949 to 1966 on a sweeping current of peace and prosperity and spending as it caught up with WWII inflation.

CHAPTER

Vietnam, Stagflation, and the Information Revolution

There has never been a commercial technology like [the Internet] in the history of the world, whereby the minute you adopt it, it forces you to think and act globally.

—Robert D. Hormats
Under Secretary of State for Economic, Energy, and Agricultural Affairs, 2009–present

Panics at the turn of the twentieth century set the stage for the economic stagnation that lasted through WWI until Germany signed the peace treaty with the United States in 1921. The crash of 1929 sparked the economic malaise that caused the Great Depression. WWII and its aftermath kept a lid on stocks until 1949. Unlike the two previous secular bear markets and restrictive economic environments, the 18-year sideways period from 1964 to 1982 was initially triggered by political turmoil at the outset of the Vietnam conflict.

Vietnam was not only a complicated conflict by historical measures, but it was also a war without a clear beginning or
ending. No declaration of war was ever asked of or granted by
Congress. The United States was involved in Vietnam from a military standpoint starting in 1950. Under the Military Assistance
and Advisory Group, the United States began sending advisors,
arms, and money to the French to support their effort in what was
then known as French Indochina to stave off communist expansion in the north as the Soviet Union and China were providing support to Ho Chi Minh. The beginning of the Eisenhower
administration marked the end of the Korean War, and with the
death of Stalin in 1953, the cold war was fully under way. By 1954
the United States had spent $1 billion in Vietnam and was fund-
ing the bulk of the cost of the war. Throughout the Eisenhower,
Kennedy, and Johnson administrations, the war escalated.

Rising Conflict, Rising Inflation

The Civil Rights Act outlawing racial discrimination and segregation passed in July 1964 and set off racial tensions that would
haunt the nation throughout the rest of the 1960s, beginning
with riots in New York City later that month. Meanwhile, in
response to a naval engagement between North Vietnam and
the United States, the Gulf of Tonkin Resolution was approved
unanimously on August 7, 1964, by the U.S. Congress, per-
mitting Lyndon B. Johnson the use of conventional military
force in Southeast Asia, marking the "official" beginning of
the Vietnam War. See Figure 8.1 for a detailed graphical look
at the Dow during Vietnam. Following Johnson's defeat of
Goldwater in the 1964 presidential election, the United States
escalated bombing in November of that year.

Regular bombing began in February 1965 and the first
U.S. combat forces arrived in Vietnam on March 8, 1965. A
few days later Federal Reserve Board Chairman Martin warned
that the economy was running a fever and could overheat.

The year 1966, when the Hirsch Organization incorporated
and conceived the *Stock Trader's Almanac*, was fraught with peril.

In May, U.S. forces commenced firing into Cambodia and the bombing of Hanoi began on June 29. With geopolitical wrangling on high in Indochina, U.S. forces in the Vietnam theater neared 500,000 by year end. In eight months, from the February 9 bull market top to the October 7 bear market bottom, the Dow dropped 25.2 percent and the S&P fell 22.2 percent.

Sharp declines ensued after hostilities ramped up and the Vietnam conflict morphed into full-blown war. As military spending grew, a double bottom formed in the Dow in August and October 1966. Johnson's approval rating fell to 44 percent before the 1966 midterm elections, and the Democrats lost 48 House seats (16.3 percent). On midterm election day, the S&P was down 12.7 percent for the year and slipped 0.5 percent further by year end. With the nation and his party divided over Vietnam, LBJ would not seek reelection in 1968.

Throughout 1967 and 1968 the stock market and the country reacted to Johnson's expansion of the war and the carnage, antiwar protests, riots, and the assassinations of Martin Luther King, Jr. and Robert Kennedy. Stock prices were flat. Government expenditure on the Vietnam War, up 50 percent from 1964 to 1968, began to heat up inflation.

The CPI was running at an annual rate of 5 percent at the end of 1968. Over the next two years during a mild bull market, the S&P 500 rallied 46.7 percent while the Dow shot up 32.4 percent from the 1966 low to the election year top in December 1968. A nine-year expansion continued, but a wartime price ceiling capped the market around S&P 100 and Dow 1,000. A year-and-a-half-long bear market that drove both the Dow and the S&P down about 36 percent pushed both indexes through their respective 1966 lows to bottoms on May 26, 1970, at Dow 631.16 and S&P 69.29, the floor of the market. As the market rebounded in 1969, the Fed began to fight inflation by increasing prime interest rates to a record high. Neil Armstrong walked on the moon. Half a million people gathered at Woodstock. And the draft was reinstated for the first time since WWII.

Protests and demonstrations against the Vietnam War, racism, repression, in support of civil rights for women and minorities, as well as on environmental issues plagued the nation in 1970, a year that marked the first Earth Day. The "Chicago Seven" were found not guilty of inciting riots at the 1968 Democratic National Convention, but five were convicted of crossing state lines with intent to do the same. U.S. forces entered Cambodia on April 30. Four students were shot and killed by National Guardsmen at a war protest at Kent State University in Ohio on May 4, and two were killed on May 15 as police fired on a demonstration at Jackson State University in Mississippi.

With Wall Street already sour on Nixon's State of the Union speech, this confluence of volatile events in the spring of 1970 drove the S&P down 25.9 percent in just four and a half months to the midterm bear market bottom on May 26. Nixon's approval held strong at 58 percent, and by midterm election day the S&P had sprung back to be only down 8.5 percent. The GOP lost only 12 House seats. The Vietnam bill started coming due and U.S. gold reserves were slowly draining.

U.S. WWII prowess helped turn the dollar into the world's reserve currency. Nixon's halt on the convertibility of gold (making the dollar a fiat currency) and the implementation of wage and price controls tipped the scales the wrong way in 1971 and pushed the market even lower. The United States continued to bomb North Vietnam heavily and inflation began to crank up.

The CPI had climbed 32.3 percent, from 93 when the Gulf of Tonkin Resolution passed in 1966 to 123 at the end of 1971, and it was now running at an annual growth rate of 4.4 percent. The prospects for peace and Nixon's reelection pushed the Dow to its war high of 1,051.70 on January 11, 1973, which would not be surpassed for 10 years. Direct U.S. involvement in the Vietnam War officially came to an end on January 27, 1973, with the signing of the Paris Peace Accords. But the war dragged on for two more years.

The year Hank Aaron hit home run 715 to break Babe Ruth's record, 1974, was shrouded on turmoil. Even though the Arab oil embargo that began on October 19, 1973, was lifted on March 18, 1974, the damage was already done, causing a severe recession in the United States that would last until 1975. Watergate scandal hearings and trials got ugly in the spring. Nixon was implicated in the cover-up of the Watergate break-in when the infamous tapes were released and was forced to resign August 9, the first U.S. president to do so.

Stocks plummeted on the news of resignation, lopping 23.0 percent off the S&P in less than two months and 27.6 percent off the Dow by December in the final plunge of the 1973–1974 bear market. This was one of the 10 worst bears since 1900. All told, the Dow lost 45.1 percent, the S&P 48.2 percent, and the young Nasdaq Composite was slashed 59.9 percent. Inflation was now up 68 percent over the past 10 years and running at an annual rate of 11 percent at the end of 1974.

But the final low of the secular bear was in and so was Yale Hirsch's "BUY!" recommendation, mailed on the day of the bottom for the S&P. Vice President Ford was sworn in as president. He pardoned Nixon on September 8 and managed to garner a 54 percent approval rating by midterm election time.

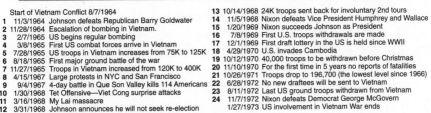

Start of Vietnam Conflict 8/7/1964
1 11/3/1964 Johnson defeats Republican Barry Goldwater
2 11/28/1964 Escalation of bombing in Vietnam.
3 2/7/1965 US begins regular bombing
4 3/8/1965 First US combat forces arrive in Vietnam
5 7/28/1965 US troops in Vietnam increases from 75K to 125K
6 8/18/1965 First major ground battle of the war
7 11/27/1965 Troops in Vietnam increased from 120K to 400K
8 4/15/1967 Large protests in NYC and San Francisco
9 9/4/1967 4-day battle in Que Son Valley kills 114 Americans
10 1/30/1968 Tet Offensive—Viet Cong surprise attacks
11 3/16/1968 My Lai massacre
12 3/31/1968 Johnson announces he will not seek re-election
13 10/14/1968 24K troops sent back for involuntary 2nd tours
14 11/5/1968 Nixon defeats Vice President Humphrey and Wallace
15 1/20/1969 Nixon succeeds Johnson as President
16 7/8/1969 First U.S. troops withdrawals are made
17 12/1/1969 First draft lottery in the US is held since WWII
18 4/29/1970 U.S. invades Cambodia
19 10/12/1970 40,000 troops to be withdrawn before Christmas
20 11/10/1970 For the first time in 5 years no reports of fatalities
21 10/26/1971 Troops drop to 196,700 (the lowest level since 1966)
22 6/28/1972 No new draftees will be sent to Vietnam
23 8/11/1972 Last US ground troops withdrawn from Vietnam
24 11/7/1972 Nixon defeats Democrat George McGovern
1/27/1973 US involvement in Vietnam War ends

FIGURE 8.1 Vietnam and the Dow

But the country was so disenchanted with the Republicans that they lost 48 House seats (25.0 percent). The last marines evacuated the embassy during the fall of Saigon on April 30, 1975. The *Mayaguez* incident in which the Khmer Rouge hijacked the U.S. merchant container ship SS *Mayaguez* in May 1975 marked the last official battle of the United States in the Vietnam War.

The Great Stagflation

When the smoke had cleared from the Bicentennial celebrations and *Viking II* landed on Mars, the bull market stopped. On September 21, 1976, after pushing the Dow up 75.7 percent from its 1974 low, the Dow topped out at 1,014.79, short of its war-high and all-time-high of 1,051.70 reached in January 1973.

OPEC increased oil prices again in December 1976. On Jimmy Carter's first day as president in January 1977, he pardoned all Vietnam draft dodgers. Carter accomplished a great deal in his one term in office. But this was arguably the most difficult time to govern since the early 1930s, and he could not shake the stigma of the economic malaise, rising energy prices, and stagflation.

An increase in Social Security taxes and a minimum wage hike in late 1977 helped facilitate the last gasp of the 1976–1978 bear. Post–Vietnam War and energy crisis inflation really began to ramp up in 1978. The CPI had continued by rising 117 percent from 93 in 1964 to 202 in 1978. Federal Reserve interest rate hikes pushed the discount rate 350 basis points higher during the year to 9.5 percent.

After falling 11.5 percent in post–election year 1977, the S&P 500 had reached a bear market bottom March 6, 1978, for a total loss of 19.4 percent and the Dow was off 26.9 percent from September 1976 to February 1978. A short six-month bull market pushed the Dow up 22.3 percent from February to September 1978. The S&P suffered a relatively mild correction of 13.6 percent over the next two months while the Dow continued to slide until the April 1980 election year bottom.

The S&P did not top out until October of pre–election year 1979. President Carter's groundbreaking September 1978 Camp David talks with Egyptian President Sadat and Israeli Premier Begin helped form a framework for the two countries' peace accord. Carter's approval rating remained at a middling 49 percent by the 1978 midterm elections as the S&P had only slipped 1.3 percent year to date. Democrats lost 15 House seats (5.1 percent) and the S&P finished the year up 1.1 percent. Carter helped engineer the peace treaty between Israel and Egypt in 1979, but geopolitical and economic conditions worsened.

The Three Mile Island disaster would put a damper on nuclear power in the United States, which could have alleviated much of our energy trials and tribulations back then— and still can. The 1979 energy crisis began when OPEC raised oil prices on July 15, the same day Carter gave his crisis of confidence speech outlining a proposal to reduce U.S. dependence on foreign oil with a 10-year, $140 billion program. Gold rallied precipitously as the Hunts began their attempt to corner the silver market. Iran seized the U.S. embassy and took hostages.

But the appointment of the caped inflation fighter, Paul Volcker, to chairman of Federal Reserve Board bolstered the economy and the country, limiting the Dow's loss to 16.4 percent during the 17-month bear market from September 1978 to April 1980. While the Dow logged a yearlong bull market until April 1981, the S&P reached a new record high of 140.52 on November 28, 1980, poking just above its 1973 high of 120.24. The Dow did not top its 1973 high until November 1982. From 1979 through 1981, sky-high inflation, record interest rates, high oil prices, the U.S. boycott of the 1980 Moscow Summer Olympics, economic sanctions on the USSR over the invasion of Afghanistan, the Iran hostage crisis, and the Hunt silver debacle forced another bear market and recession that would both end in midterm 1982. The gross national product fell 1.8 percent in 1982, the worst decline since 1946. Unemployment reached 10.8 percent in November 1982, its highest level since the Depression. It was an ugly decade for investors, but sustained inflation and low stock valuations had put the market in position for a comeback.

The Information Age

Computations and arithmetic processes were performed by the ancients for thousands of years on tools like the abacus. During the first 2,000 years of the modern era, mechanical computing devices evolved from the astronomical clock to slide rules. According to the *Oxford English Dictionary*, the word *computer* was first used in 1613 to describe a "person who carried out calculations or computations."

The paper punch card loom in 1801 led to Herman Hollerith's Tabulating Machine Company in 1896, which became the core of the company that would change its name to International Business Machines (IBM) in 1924. The first electronic computers were developed during WWII between 1940 and 1945. IBM and the "Seven Dwarfs" (Burroughs, UNIVAC, NCR, Control Data, Honeywell, RCA, and GE) produced mainframes from the late 1950s through the 1970s. But it was not until the 1960s and early 1970s that the seeds of the Internet, the personal computer, and the Information Age were planted with the development of programmable computer language, packet switching, and integrated circuit microprocessors. These developments would serve as the enabling technology that powered the greatest super boom in market history, beginning in 1982 and ending in 2000, fittingly, with the dot-com crash.

In his book, *A Programming Language* (Wiley, 1962), Kenneth E. Iverson describes how he invented the mathematical notations while at Harvard that would later be used in IBM systems when he worked there in the early 1960s. ARPANET and the TCP/IP Internet protocol were first developed in 1969. When Intel's first general-purpose commercial 4004 microprocessor was shipped in 1971, the roots of the information boom took hold.

Over the next decade the personal computer evolved from Hewlett-Packard's BASIC programmable computer to the Apple IIe, released in January 1983. Microsoft launched MS-DOS in IBM PCs in 1982 at the same time the stock market launched its stratospheric rise. In a 1989 speech to the Computer Science Club at the University of Waterloo in Canada, Bill Gates said, "in 1981 . . . a move from 64K to 640K felt like something that would last a great deal of time. Well, it didn't—it took about only 6 years before people started to see that as a real problem." In 1984 Michael Dell founded Dell, the company that would fuel the proliferation of the PC and support the super boom.

Constant improvements in software, operating systems, graphical user interfaces, and an explosion of networking capacity and steadily declining prices made these enabling technologies readily available to everybody. Then, the Internet. AOL launched its dedicated online service in 1985 and the World Wide Web was born in 1992, sending the stock market into outer space. Cellular phones and wireless technology inflated the speculative bubble to the breaking point. The greatest super boom ever seen ended in 2000 with the dot-com crash.

It remains to be seen what's lurking in research labs and garages around the world in 2010 that will enable the next super boom. What is certain is that things are lurking. In the final chapter of this book, I venture a few thoughts as to where the next new, new things may come from and propose a few investment ideas to take advantage of them.

Politics Paves the Way

Amazingly, after keeping them in captivity for 444 days, Iran freed the U.S. hostages on Ronald Reagan's first day in office, January 20, 1981. Reagan proclaimed that we were in the "worst economic mess since the Depression" and promised to cut taxes and reduce the deficit. He succeeded in implementing tax cuts and policy initiatives and provided unwavering leadership that stiffened the resolve of the nation, shored up the economy, and allowed business to flourish.

In his landmark book, *The Coming Boom: Economic, Political and Social* (Simon & Schuster, 1982), Herman Kahn (aka Dr. Strangelove) of the Hudson Institute made some astute and prescient observations that are just as applicable in 2010 as they were in 1982:

> *Information revolution.* There have been enormous increases in the productivity of both goods and service industries as the direct result of new computer, communications, and sensor technologies (for example, networking, information processing, CAD/CAM and other automation of the office, factory, and home). This also encourages capital investment both directly and indirectly.

> *Other new technologies.* Many creative developments in biotechnologies, space, new materials, and other "high tech" industries, plus heavy capital investment in traditional technologies which are now becoming more cost effective—for example, environmental protection, better transportation, and the more efficient use of energy.

> *Positive self-fulfilling prophecies....* should help create greater general confidence and more inspiring "visions of the future." This should lead to restoration of what Keynes called the "animal spirits" of businessmen, entrepreneurs, and investors and lessen (at least for a decade or two) "social limits to growth."[1]

> [Economists] are focusing on issues of increased savings, economic efficiency, market incentives, rational taxa-

---

[1]Herman Kahn, *The Coming Boom: Economic, Political and Social* (New York: Simon & Schuster, 1982), 16.

tion and expenditures, reduced and more appropriate welfare, and so on.[2]

There are many possibilities for flexibility, ingenuity, and creativity (as well as for basic reforms) in dealing with the 1980s and 1990s. This is true in economics, defense, technology, and ideology—all areas where the administration is taking new initiatives.[3]

We have barely begun to see the sort of political and ideological changes that were gathering momentum in 1982. Policy initiatives identical to those employed in the 1980s will not work in the future, but new ones in the same spirit of solving the problems and issues at hand will.

The Lesser Impact of Boom-Time Wars

Significant conflicts came and went during the information super boom. None had a major impact on the market. The most significant of these was the first Gulf War. Like the Korean War, the Persian Gulf War of 1990 and 1991 was a major international military campaign that was instigated by the unilateral invasion of one country by another.

After an unprovoked Iraq took over a sovereign U.N. member nation, a global trade embargo was imposed, and Iraq was given until January 15, 1991, to withdraw from Kuwait. See Figure 8.2 for a detailed graphical look at the Dow during the Gulf War. Military intervention was authorized as the United States, NATO, Persian Gulf states, and other nations from around the world amassed nearly 1 million coalition forces around Iraq and Kuwait. The world stood shoulder-to-shoulder in defense of Kuwait. Under then–Chairman of the Joint Chiefs Colin Powell's doctrine of overwhelming force,

---

[2]Kahn, *The Coming Boom*, 19.
[3]Kahn, *The Coming Boom*, 27.

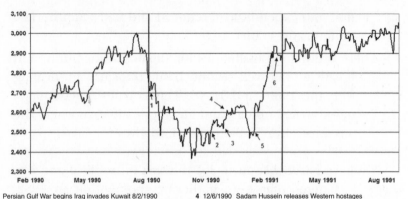

Persian Gulf War begins Iraq invades Kuwait 8/2/1990
1   8/6/1990   The UN orders a global trade embargo against Iraq
2   11/11/1990   UN gives Iraq until Jan 15 to withdrawal from Kuwait
3   11/29/1990   UN authorizes military intervention

4   12/6/1990   Sadam Hussein releases Western hostages
5   1/16/1991   Operation Desert Storm begins
6   2/23/1991   Ground-phase of the war begins
Persian Gulf War ends Iraq retreats Pres Bush orders cease-fire 2/27/1991

FIGURE 8.2   Dow and the Gulf War

Operation Desert Storm was the swiftest, least lethal, and least costly military engagement.

Actual combat operations lasted a mere six weeks with the ground phase taking only four days for the United States and allies to defeat Iraq and liberate Kuwait on February 27, 1991. While we were all mesmerized by the almost surreal news conferences and video play-by-play of the war by Powell and Coalition Commander General Norman Schwarzkopf, this event had little lasting impact on the economy, the market, or inflation.

Longest Bull Market

The USSR began to break up in early 1990 and the savings and loan crisis came to a close. Following the first Gulf War, an eight-month recession ended in March 1991 and the longest bull market in history continued its historic march. Though no bottom or bear market ever occurred, a loss of 1.5 percent in the S&P in 1994 would serve as a launching pad for banner market gains over the next five years.

President Clinton was reelected in 1996 with 49 percent to Dole's 41 percent of the popular vote as stocks blasted right past Fed Chairman Greenspan's famous irrational exuberance speech in December 1996. Whitewater investigations and the Lewinsky affair tainted Clinton administration dealings, yet the "Teflon" president maintained high approval ratings in 1998. Clinton was impeached in December but acquitted the following February.

The year 1998 was a year of mega-mergers. The American Stock Exchange and Nasdaq wed, as did Exxon and Mobil. The Asian currency flu and the collapse of the Russian ruble created a global currency crisis and caused the shortest bear market on record—the Dow dropping 19.3 percent in 45 days in the summer of 1998. Renowned currency hedge fund Long Term Capital Management was caught in the carnage, and the Fed engineered a $3.5 billion bailout—a precursor of bailouts yet to come. A double bottom formed in August and October ahead of the final run to the 2000 top.

In the final stage of the super boom, tech IPOs and day trading inflated the dot-com stock bubble to historic proportions. The Dow closed the last day of 1999 at a record high of 11,497.12. Little did Yale or anyone else, for that matter, realize in 1976 that the Dow would wind up blowing through his

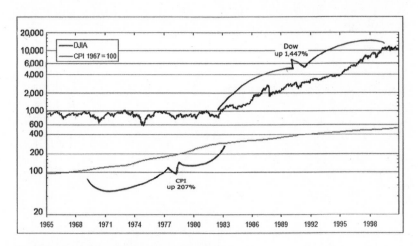

FIGURE 8.3   DJIA over CPI, 1965–2000
Sources: Stock Trader's Almanac; www.bls.gov.

500 percent prediction and making a 1,957 percent move from the Vietnam low to the 2000 dot-com bubble high! As you can see in Figure 8.3, from the intraday low on August 11, 1982, at 770, the Dow climbed 1,447 percent to an intraday high of 11,908.50 18 years later. Two weeks after the turn of the millennium, on January 14, 2000, the greatest super boom in history came to an end. It may turn out to be the biggest super boom ever experienced, but it won't be the last.

PART IV

THE PRODIGAL PATTERN RETURNS

Moses Shapiro (of General Instrument) told me, "Son, this is Talmudic wisdom. Always ask the question 'If not?' Few people have good strategies for when their assumptions are wrong." That's the best business advice I ever got.
—John Malone, *Fortune*, 2/16/98

Throughout these pages a plethora of historical data has been presented to support the prediction of Dow 38,820 by 2025. In order to make this seemingly wild call in such difficult times, historical patterns and cycles have been observed and molded into a forecast. As a reader, you are not required to believe in a new and mystical valuation model or demographic study projection. You only need to believe that stocks respond to inflation—the very same inflation that you witness each time you visit a supermarket or fill your tank.

Sources and causes of inflation are open to debate, but its existence is not. Throughout history, sharp rises in inflation have resulted in even sharper rises in equity markets: 100 percent during and after WWI, 75 percent immediately following WWII, and a 200 percent rise surrounding the Vietnam conflict all resulted in super booms for the Dow.

But inflation alone cannot trigger a boom. A new innovation or breakthrough is needed. Henry Ford spawned mass production in the 1920s. WWII triggered a baby boom and the suburbanization of the United States, plus aviation developments substantially shrunk the size of the planet. And from the ashes of the 1970s' stagflation arose the microprocessor, predecessor of the personal computer, the cell phone, the Internet, and instant global communication.

Our aging population is not a handicap, it is an opportunity. Biotech and pharmaceutical companies know this and are working night and day to meet the needs of a shifting demographic. Personal electronics are hungry for power and as a society we are becoming increasingly aware of the detrimental effects of hydrocarbon use. Cheap, clean, and renewable energy demands will continue to grow.

All that said, exogenous events could accelerate or delay the Dow's arrival at 38,820. Inventions, innovations, and cures to modern problems could be unearthed any day. Terrorism remains a global threat. None of these events can be forecast. However, many millennia of human nature triumphing over adversity are worth betting on. DJIA 38,820 by 2025 is not a market forecast; it is an expectation that human ingenuity will overcome, as it has on countless past occasions throughout history.

CHAPTER 9

Inflation

We may face more inflation pressure than currently shows up in formal data.
— William Poole, president, Federal Reserve Bank,
St. Louis, June 2006

Throughout this book I have laid out the calculus for a super boom forecast: the combination of peacetime, supportive government policies, ubiquitous technology, and inflation.

The wars in Iraq and Afghanistan appear likely to continue for several years. If Obama remains in power, his scheduled troop withdrawals will lessen the impact of the war on the markets.

Politics swung to the Right for eight years, and lax oversight of the market and economy allowed asset bubbles to swell with reckless abandon, resulting in a crisis, a nasty recession, and a massive loss of capital in a devastating bear market. For the last two years government policy has taken a jump back to the Left. But after the 2010 midterm elections, conservative victories, and Republicans retaking control of the House, affairs of the nation have begun to shift back toward the center.

In the first real policy compromise of his still young presidency, President Obama has wisely chosen not to battle his Republican counterparts and made the deal to extend the Bush tax cuts for two years. If Obama wants to have any chance at another term, he has to win back the glowing support of his base that he had on the campaign trail and increase his popularity and approval ratings among independents and conservatives.

The third year of a president's term has historically followed the same pattern. In order to win reelection the president begins campaigning from the Oval Office with stimulating legislation and rhetoric. The year 2011 is a prepresidential election year, and the Obama political team is well aware that they will need to reinvigorate their supporters if he is going to have a shot at a second term. This political maneuvering is a major reason there has not been a Dow loss in a prepresidential election year since war-torn 1939. Since 1975, when Congress and the presidency are controlled by opposing parties or there is a split Congress, the market is usually a beneficiary.

Enabling technology is another crucial piece of the boom equation. Ideas and thoughts on a global cultural paradigm shift that could fuel the next super boom are addressed in the final chapter, including some investment strategies.

The final variable in the boom equation is inflation. As Ben Bernanke and the Federal Reserve battle deflation, I contend hidden inflation is already brewing.

The Consumer Price Index (CPI), the most widely followed and cited measure of inflation, is a somewhat dubious and suspect measuring tool and does not give the most accurate reading. The CPI has been criticized almost since its inception. The critics are often dubbed "conspiracy theorists" by economists and politicos. The crux of the argument against the CPI is that it masks inflation so governments don't have to raise taxes while they are in power. I have argued that inflation is a natural result of heightened government spending from war, financial crises, and fiscal stimulus. But the economy, and the world, is ever changing. Looking at inflation the same way we did 10 years ago or two wars ago does not accurately reflect real-world inflation in this country.

Having a CPI number is a fine idea, but the methodology needs to be reassessed from time to time. There is indeed precedent for this. There have been six comprehensive revisions to the CPI since its inception. Looking at the changes and the catalysts for those changes paints a worrisome picture. The shifts in power at the White House, performance on Wall Street, and the man at the helm of the Federal Reserve have shaped the CPI's destiny. It may be time again to reassess its usefulness.

Creation of the CPI

The federal government realized that it needed a measure of inflation during World War I. A variable number needed to be created to account for inflation so the government could annually adjust its employees' salaries by a cost of living adjustment (COLA).

If inflation were high, federal workers would receive a larger annual raise than if it were low. For example, a clerk working at the Department of Defense makes $50,000. If inflation were 2 percent, the COLA would be 2 percent, thus next year the clerk would earn $51,000. If inflation were 4 percent, the clerk would make $52,000, and so on.

The CPI was first calculated in 1921 using a consumer expenditure survey conducted from 1917 to 1919. Although the level of sophistication has advanced over the past eight decades, the basic tenet of the CPI remains the same. The Bureau of Labor Statistics (BLS) determines how much people consume by surveying consumers in specified industrial centers. These data determine the weightings of each item used in the survey. The BLS then plugs the data into the index to calculate the average rise or decline of prices over time paid by consumers for goods and services. The survey reveals, for example, how many eggs are bought by a household.

In 1921, there were six major groups of products: food, clothing, rent, fuel, furnishings, and the ever popular miscellaneous. Once the index was created, they calculated it back to 1913.

At the time of its creation, the economy was entrenched in a deep recession and the Dow was mired in a bear market. Post–World War I expansion had ground to a halt and inflation was rampant. Inflation, as determined by the new CPI, was near 25 percent in June 1920, as shown in Figure 9.1. After the calculations were in, by June 1921, inflation plummeted below negative 15 percent!

W. P. G. Harding was near the end of his relatively short tenure as the Federal Reserve chairman and Warren Harding (no relation) was at the beginning of his abbreviated two years as president. There was an obvious problem with the calculation of the CPI. Consumer prices simply do not swing an average of 40 percent in a year's time. But this was a start and better than nothing.

First Comprehensive Revision

In 1940, war drums were pounding in Europe. The United States was recovering from the Great Depression. FDR was at the height of his power, and the Fed was chaired by Marriner S. Eccles. Having ascended to the chairmanship in 1934, Eccles was part of the leadership that got this country back to work and the economy back on its feet.

Attempting to stave off the inevitable war-driven inflation, it was determined that the CPI should be revised for the first time in almost 20 years. The Tennessee Valley Authority, a corporation owned by the U.S. government and founded in 1933 during the Great Depression, however, changed the playing field. There were significantly more employees on the government's payroll, and COLAs began to equate to big dollars.

The first comprehensive revision was more of a tweak than a revision. A new consumer expenditure survey was implemented based on 1934–1936 and the scope was expanded from 32 cities to 34. Inflation was in check and the economy was flourishing. After the revisions were implemented, inflation ran up from nearly 0 percent to the low teens in 1942— another example of the impact of war on inflation. The Dow in turn got hammered, bottoming out in April 1942. The markets then caught up with inflation and more than doubled over the next four years—the beginning of the post-WWII super boom.

Second Comprehensive Revision

In 1953, newly elected President Eisenhower inherited a robust economy and the markets were soaring. The Korean War ended in July 1953 and inflation was contained. William Martin had just taken over as the top economist at the Fed.

During the 17 years since the first CPI revision, various "improvements" were made. In 1951, seven cities had their consumer expenditures adjusted and the 1950 census was factored in. Adjustments were made in the calculation to remove "new unit bias" caused by rent control. Housing has always been the most weighted and controversial factor in CPI calculations, and efforts have continually been made to account for it. New items such as televisions and frozen food were added to the list of consumables.

The second comprehensive revision also added small and medium-sized cities. This was a major change as until then, only the largest cities in the country were surveyed. But the 1950s saw an increase in automobile ownership and suburbanization. The Bureau of Labor Statistics also decided to include central cities with attached urban areas. This is an excellent example of how the CPI must be changed periodically to reflect the changing lifestyles of consumers.

In addition, the BLS refined the target population for the survey to include clerical workers. New data collection capabilities allowed for an improvement in pricing and calculation methods. The list of items was updated and restaurant meals were now included. After the adjustment, the economy fell into recession. Inflation dipped into negative territory in 1954 and stayed there for a year. The markets, however, were unfazed. After a minor bear market, they pressed higher.

Third Comprehensive Revision

The year 1964 was the beginning of turbulent times for the United States. The assassination of President Kennedy and the buildup to war in Vietnam had the county on edge. Inflation had been almost unchanged for the better part of a decade, but things were changing, and this was a chance to check inflation before war spending caused major inflation as it had in decades past.

But how to prevent it? The war couldn't be stopped on account of inflationary concerns. And as history tells us, war and inflation are inevitable cause and effect. If the cause can't be altered, then the effect must. Thus, further revisions to the CPI.

William Martin sat atop the Federal Reserve from 1951 to 1970 and was in charge during the second comprehensive review. This time, another major policy change was implemented that reflected the changing population of the country: single-person households were added to the target population. Until then, only families were included, but it was recognized that people were beginning to stay single longer and had much different consumption habits than families.

Inflation started to creep up in 1966 but remained in check for the duration of Vietnam, until 1973. A litany of exogenous influences on the U.S. economy, especially the Arab oil embargo and Watergate, caused inflation to surge into the low teens and the market tanked.

Fourth Comprehensive Revision

It had only been 14 years since the last revision, and President Carter was struggling through his inflation-plagued and energy-starved presidency. The Fed chairmanship had changed hands twice from William Martin to Arthur Burns to William Miller. Instability and the absence of one salient, confident voice at the Fed spelled trouble for the market and economy.

Not much had improved since 1973. There were muted bull markets and the economy was in expansion, but inflation remained a major problem. It was not until Paul Volcker took the helm of the Fed in 1979 that the economy found sure footing. It could be argued that the improvements to the CPI made under Volcker's tutelage played a major role in the 1982–2000 super bull market for stocks. The inflation rate had come down from double digits, but was on the rise again. Something had to be done to fight a surge in inflation, so the BLS made the most radical and controversial round of changes to date.

First, they created a new CPI for all urban consumers. They also expanded the sample significantly, increasing the pricing frequency from quarterly to bimonthly. They introduced new methods and lists. They implemented new probabilities and checklists. Many contend this made the CPI a set of massaged data. After the revision, inflation surged to around 15 percent before drifting steadily downward to under 5 percent.

Fifth Comprehensive Revision

It was 1987 and Alan Greenspan was chairman of the Fed. Inflation was muted, but there was a growing sense of concern about the health of the U.S. economy as a whole. There hadn't been a recession since the double-dip in 1980–1981. The rise of Asian markets proved to be a burden on the domestic economy as automakers and electronics, two stalwarts of the U.S. economy, began to be imported at higher rates.

The CPI, once again, had to be reassessed. Reagan was at the height of his second-term resurgence and the stock market was booming. The revisions included a housing survey redesign. An introduction of new technologies made the CPI more efficient. Inflation held below 5 percent for the most part.

Sixth Comprehensive Revision

By 1998, the economy was roaring and Greenspan was a legend. Moreover, the technological advances of the country and the shift to a service-based economy had once again changed the playing field. With computers and technology at their disposal and carte blanche from the White House, the Federal Reserve and the BLS ushered in a new era of economics.

They once again implemented a new housing index estimation system, added new surveys and data collection techniques, and extensively revised the item classification system. The CPI has been tweaked and revised quite substantially since the 1998 revision with changes made practically on the fly.

Current CPI

Inflation is now permanently muted. In fact, as you can see in Figure 9.1, the range of inflation is so tight that it was in a 4 percent range for 15 years! It had not gone above 5 percent or below 1 percent from March 1991 until July 2008. Even then it peaked at 5.5 percent. One year later it bottomed in July at 2.0 percent.

From an exponential commodity boom through a financial crisis, the range only expanded to 7.5 percent. Several improvements have been made since 1998, including a new housing survey, a new formula that reflects shifts in consumer spending, a replacement of sample items in the personal computer and other categories, an increase in the sample size of

FIGURE 9.1 **Consumer Price Index, 1914–2010**

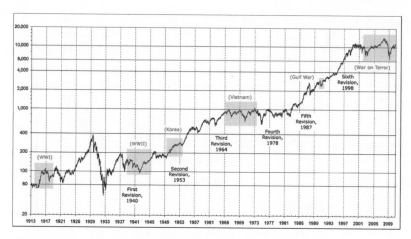

FIGURE 9.2   DJIA and Major CPI Revisions, 1913–2009
Source: © Stock Trader's Almanac.

the Consumer Expenditure Survey, and an expanded collection of price data to all business days of the month. What began as a simple calculation of consumer prices has swollen to a Frankenstein-style creation. Figure 9.2 shows the timeline of the major revisions to the CPI alongside the chart of the Dow.

Every bit of sampled data is confidential. The computers now collect data in unprecedented quantities, none of which are in the public domain. The methodologies are convoluted. In some cases they are arcane, in others they are unrealistic. Perhaps this explains why the Fed has chosen personal consumption expenditures as its preferred inflation gauge, although this indicator is dependent on actual spending. During a recession, incomes, and thereby spending, are lower.

A Different Tale

Since September 11, 2001, through the most recent November reading of the CPI, the inflation index is up a meager 23 percent. Having made numerous trips to the market and gas station over the past decade, it is simply unimaginable that prices are only up 23 percent. Energy costs have doubled, if not tripled. Medical costs have skyrocketed.

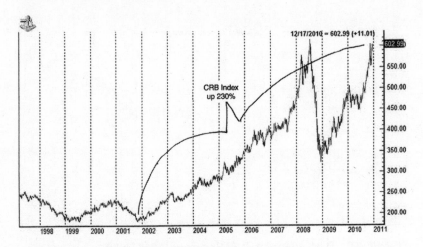

FIGURE 9.3   NYFE CRB Index (Weekly)
Source: TradeNavigator.com © 1999–2010. All rights reserved.

The price of an ounce of gold (in U.S. dollars) and the New York Futures Exchange Commodity Research Bureau (NYFE CRB) Index are better indicators of the prices consumers actually pay for daily necessities. (See Figures 9.3 and 9.4.)

Since 2001 gold is up 402 percent and the CRB is up 230 percent. Much of these moves could be in response to a weakening

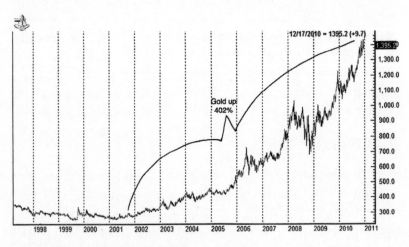

FIGURE 9.4   Gold Comex Weekly
Source: TradeNavigator.com © 1999–2010. All rights reserved.

dollar. From its July 2001 peak to the November 2009 low, the U.S. Dollar Index (USDX) had shed nearly 40 percent of its purchasing power—another strong argument that inflation is much higher than the CPI calculated 23 percent.

The Fed's balance sheet expansion from less than $1 trillion in 2008 to the current level of over $2 trillion (and growing) is a wild card. If the Fed is able to unload the assets that have been purchased before they mature, total money will not be impacted much. A persistently weak economic recovery could force the Fed to supply even more liquidity. Much of this liquidity is currently being held at the Fed in the form of excess reserves, but at some point in the future, banks may begin to seek other places to put this capital to work. It is currently earning 0.25 percent per year in interest, not a very attractive return.

Hedging Inflation

As we wind down our major military presence in Iraq and Afghanistan, the war bill will come due, generating even more inflation, hidden or evident. The most important question with respect to inflation is not if or when inflation will heat up, or by how much, but what is the best hedge against inflation.

When the economic recovery gains traction over the next several years, it will be the stock market that moves to new heights, not gold or other safe havens. In Figure 9.5, a hypothetical $1,000 was invested in the Dow and gold at the high, low, and close of each year since 1975 when active trading in gold began. The table shows stock's clear advantage over gold over the long haul.

Since 1975, stocks have been a clear winner. Gold's performance only worsens when the cost of storage and/or trading fees are taken into consideration. The performance of stocks only improves with the inclusion of dividends (left out in this calculation). Most striking is the advantage stocks displayed from 1980 to 1999. During this 20-year time frame, when the CPI more than doubled, the inflation-adjusted Dow was up 444 percent versus a 22 percent loss for inflation-adjusted gold.

Since 2000, as the U.S. Dollar Index (USDX) has fallen briskly, gold has handily outperformed stocks. With gold at

Returns of $1,000 Annual Investment in DJIA vs. Gold Compared to Inflation since 1975

	Dow Jones Industrial Average						Gold Futures					
	High	Low	Year	$1,000 Invested In DJIA			$1,000 Invested In Gold			High	Low	Year
Year	Close	Close	Close	@High	@Low	@Yearend	@High	@Low	@Yearend	Close	Close	Close
1975	881.81	632.04	852.41	1.13	1.58	1.17	5.33	7.62	7.09	187.7	131.2	141.0
1976	1,014.79	858.71	1,004.65	0.99	1.16	1.00	7.08	9.73	7.37	141.2	102.8	135.7
1977	999.75	800.85	831.17	1.00	1.25	1.20	5.92	7.84	5.97	168.9	127.6	167.5
1978	907.74	742.12	805.01	1.10	1.35	1.24	4.05	5.95	4.37	247.0	168.0	229.0
1979	897.61	796.67	838.74	1.11	1.26	1.19	1.85	4.57	1.85	541.0	218.6	541.0
1980	1,000.17	759.13	963.99	1.00	1.32	1.04	1.20	2.08	1.67	834.0	480.0	599.5
1981	1,024.05	824.01	875.00	0.98	1.21	1.14	1.65	2.52	2.48	605.0	397.2	402.8
1982	1,070.55	776.92	1,046.54	0.93	1.29	0.96	2.01	3.32	2.21	497.0	301.5	453.0
1983	1,287.20	1,027.04	1,258.64	0.78	0.97	0.79	1.93	2.66	2.58	518.2	376.3	388.0
1984	1,286.64	1,086.57	1,211.57	0.78	0.92	0.83	2.46	3.23	3.23	407.3	309.2	309.7
1985	1,553.10	1,184.96	1,546.67	0.64	0.84	0.65	2.88	3.52	3.02	347.3	284.1	331.1
1986	1,955.57	1,502.29	1,895.95	0.51	0.67	0.53	2.25	3.04	2.46	445.2	328.9	406.9
1987	2,722.42	1,738.74	1,938.83	0.37	0.58	0.52	1.99	2.53	2.05	502.0	394.9	488.9
1988	2,183.50	1,879.14	2,168.57	0.46	0.53	0.46	2.05	2.51	2.43	488.2	399.2	412.3
1989	2,791.41	2,144.64	2,753.20	0.36	0.47	0.36	2.35	2.76	2.47	425.0	362.0	405.2
1990	2,999.75	2,365.10	2,633.66	0.33	0.42	0.38	2.34	2.86	2.52	427.5	349.8	396.2
1991	3,168.83	2,470.30	3,168.83	0.32	0.40	0.32	2.47	2.87	2.82	404.5	348.2	355.2
1992	3,413.21	3,136.58	3,301.11	0.29	0.32	0.30	2.75	3.03	3.00	363.2	330.1	333.1
1993	3,794.33	3,241.95	3,754.09	0.26	0.31	0.27	2.43	3.06	2.55	411.3	326.9	391.9
1994	3,978.36	3,593.35	3,834.44	0.25	0.28	0.26	2.49	2.69	2.60	401.4	372.1	384.4
1995	5,216.47	3,832.08	5,117.12	0.19	0.26	0.20	2.51	2.69	2.58	397.8	372.2	388.1
1996	6,560.91	5,032.94	6,448.27	0.15	0.20	0.16	2.39	2.71	2.71	417.7	369.2	369.2
1997	8,259.31	6,391.69	7,908.25	0.12	0.16	0.13	2.73	3.51	3.45	366.6	284.8	289.9
1998	9,374.27	7,539.07	9,181.43	0.11	0.13	0.11	3.17	3.60	3.46	315.8	277.9	289.2
1999	11,497.12	9,120.67	11,497.12	0.09	0.11	0.09	3.07	3.94	3.45	326.0	253.9	289.6
2000	11,722.98	9,796.03	10,786.85	0.09	0.10	0.09	3.14	3.77	3.65	318.7	265.3	273.6
2001	11,337.92	8,235.81	10,021.50	0.09	0.12	0.10	3.39	3.90	3.58	294.8	256.6	279.0
2002	10,635.25	7,286.27	8,341.63	0.09	0.14	0.12	2.86	3.59	2.87	349.7	278.5	348.2
2003	10,453.92	7,524.06	10,453.92	0.10	0.13	0.10	2.40	3.10	2.40	417.2	322.2	416.1
2004	10,854.54	9,749.99	10,783.01	0.09	0.10	0.09	2.18	2.67	2.28	457.8	374.9	438.4
2005	10,940.55	10,012.36	10,717.50	0.09	0.10	0.09	1.88	2.41	1.93	531.5	414.3	518.9
2006	12,510.57	10,667.39	12,463.15	0.08	0.09	0.08	1.39	1.89	1.57	721.5	527.8	638.0
2007	14,164.53	12,050.41	13,264.82	0.07	0.08	0.08	1.19	1.65	1.19	842.7	606.9	838.0
2008	13,058.20	7,552.29	8,776.39	0.08	0.13	0.11	1.00	1.42	1.13	1,004.3	705.0	884.3
2009	10,548.51	6,547.05	10,428.05	0.09	0.15	0.10	0.82	1.24	0.91	1,218.3	807.3	1,096.2
2010	11,444.08	9,686.48	11,370.06 *	0.09	0.10	—	0.71	0.95	—	1,416.1	1,052.8	1,392.1 *
	Total Units DJIA*			15.21	19.14	16.23	92.30	121.42	101.89	Total Ounces Gold*		
	Current Value*			$172,943	$217,655	$184,577	$128,491	$169,035	$141,847			
	Total Investment*			$36,000	$36,000	$35,000	$36,000	$36,000	$35,000			
	Total Return*			380.4%	504.6%	427.4%	256.9%	369.5%	305.3%			
	CPI (1982–1984=100) Dec 1974 to October 2010						51.9	218.9	322%			

Returns of $1,000 Annual Investment in DJIA vs. Gold Compared to Inflation 1980–1999

	Total Units DJIA*			8.92	11.39	9.47	47.12	59.12	53.72	Total Ounces Gold*		
	Current Value*			$102,543	$130,914	$108,854	$13,647	$17,121	$15,558			
	Total Investment*			$20,000	$20,000	$20,000	$20,000	$20,000	$20,000			
	Total Return*			412.7%	554.6%	444.3%	-31.8%	-14.4%	-22.2%			
	CPI (1982–1984=100) Dec 1979 to Dec 1999						76.7	168.3	119%			

Returns of $1,000 Annual Investment in DJIA vs. Gold Compared to Inflation since 2000

	Total Units DJIA*			0.96	1.26	0.96	20.95	26.59	21.53	Total Ounces Gold*		
	Current Value*			$10,870	$14,340	$10,910	$29,161	$37,018	$29,967			
	Total Investment*			$11,000	$11,000	$10,000	$11,000	$11,000	$10,000			
	Total Return*			-1.2%	30.4%	9.1%	165.1%	236.5%	199.7%			
	CPI (1982–1984=100) Dec 1999 to October 2010						168.8	218.9	30%			

*As of 12/9/2010. Gold Data Source: Pinnacle Data Corp. Nonadjusted, continuously linked near-term contracts

FIGURE 9.5 DJIA versus Gold against Inflation

record highs and the market below its all-time high and in the midst of a potential recovery, shifting from gold to stocks could prove quite profitable once again.

Perhaps our esteemed colleague, Bill Staton, CFA, chairman of Staton Financial Advisors, who has managed money for 40 years, said it best in his September 2009 private client letter:

> Ever since the Federal Reserve Board was founded in 1913, the growth in the money supply has outstripped the growth of the economy....So long as money continues to grow faster than the economy (recently it's grown at an unprecedented rate), our currency will continue to weaken. And as it does, inflation will remain a threat to everyone's financial well being. Whatever you do with your investments... put much higher inflation at the top of your list of obstacles to overcome. If none of the above makes sense to keep up with and beat inflation, at least don't buy gold or silver. Buy U.S. forever postage stamps instead. The price of a first-class stamp has modestly outpaced inflation for decades. Plus, stamps are ultra-liquid, and they'll always be in demand.[1]

The Coming Boom

Annual Dow Jones Industrial Average earnings are on course to eclipse their previous record highs (see Figure 9.6). Cost cutting and substantial gains in productivity have enabled this brisk recovery. When consumer spending and business activity improve, increases in revenue will flow quickly to the bottom line, earnings.

The War on Terror may never end, but despite continuing violence in Iraq and Afghanistan, U.S. troop withdrawals

---

[1]Staton Financial Private Client Letter #138, September 14, 2009. Reprinted with permission.

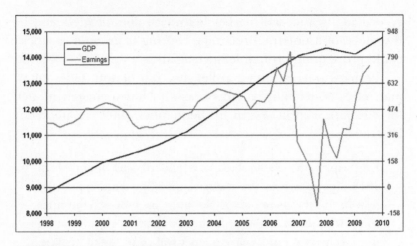

FIGURE 9.6   GDP and DJIA Annual Earnings
Sources: Barron's Statistical Department; www.bls.gov.

remain on schedule. There may be some delays as the pace of the withdrawals is adjusted in response to conditions on the ground, but combat troops left Iraq on schedule this summer and the force was reduced down to 50,000 mostly support personnel. Resolution on the formation of a new Iraqi government and a continued diminishing role of violence and chaos in that country is necessary before we can be convinced that the United States will be able to stick to the plan of having all combat troops out of Iraq by the end of 2011.

Afghan President Hamid Karzai and NATO have been at odds recently, putting political and military progress in Afghanistan in jeopardy. But U.S. troop reductions in Afghanistan remain on schedule to begin in July 2011. Delays due to the political process and operational setbacks will likely alter the actual withdrawal dates and sizes, but the trend and plan remain clear: We intend to disengage. Peacetime is the crucial component of the next Super Boom, and I expect that within the next several years, major combat operations in Afghanistan will be over, opening the door for peacetime and the accompanying super boom.

We are still at war with government spending, a trend I expect to continue for some time. The austerity movement has gained traction in parts of Europe as sovereign debt remains a looming concern, but the White House continues to spend and avoid cutbacks. From a historical perspective, government spending has always led to massive jumps in inflation. This process will happen again over the next several years as spending continues. Figure 9.7 compares the annual percentage changes in U.S. government spending (outlays) to inflation (CPI). In the 1953–2009 chart, there is a recent pop in

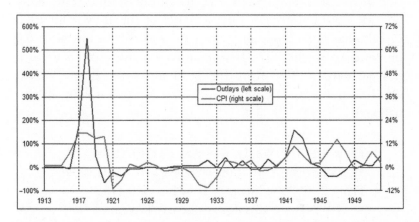

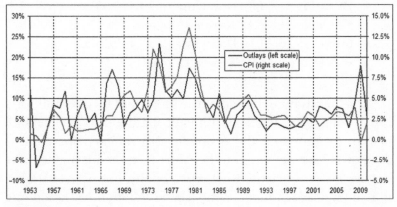

FIGURE 9.7 CPI Annual Percentage Change (1913–1952, 1953–2010)
Sources: Office of Management and Budget, www.budget.gov; Bureau of Labor Statistics, www.bls.gov.

spending. I contend that inflation will be right behind it over the next few years as it has in years past.

38,820 and Beyond

From 1974, it took eight years for the boom to start and then another eight to move up 500 percent. A 500 percent rise in the Dow over 16 years from the intraday low of 6,470 on March 6, 2009, would put the Dow at 38,820 in 2025.

Given the current Dow around 11,500, this number sounds ridiculous. But mathematically, it's quite sound. The compounded annual growth rate (CAGR) of the Dow from 1900 to 1999 has been 5 percent; from 1950 to 1999 it has been 6.6 percent. From the 1974 bottom through the end of 1999, it was 8.6 percent, and from the 1974 low to 3,420 in 1992, it was 10.8 percent. The move to 38,820 by 2020 is right in this ballpark.

- From 12/31/1999 Dow close of 11,497.12
  - 4.8 percent CAGR over 26 years to 12/31/2025
- From 3/6/2009 intraday Dow low of 6,470
  - 11.2 percent CAGR over nearly 17 years
- From 12/31/2009 Dow close of 10,428.05
  - 8.6 percent CAGR over 16 years
- From 12/16/2010 Dow close of 11,499.25
  - 8.4 percent CAGR over 15 years

It is important to note that the scope and focus of this forecast is long-term. It will be difficult for the next secular bull market to start until the major foreign military operation is over, or at least perceived to be. Moreover, the inevitable inflationary cycle associated with super booms has not yet started to rear its head. In history, war-related inflation has lasted one year for World War I, a year and a half for World War II, and almost two decades for Vietnam! The secular bull will not start until inflation returns to our economy and has time to level off, allowing for growth and innovation.

What is evident is that all the elements of the 500 percent equation are in place: a diminishing war effort, a coming period of peace, high government spending, and the likelihood of significant inflation. As the saying goes, nothing is certain. But as history has repeatedly demonstrated, there are big, identifiable patterns in the stock market, and when the right variables are added together over the right period of time, the resulting effect is a super boom the likes of which we have seen many times before. The question now is not will a super boom happen, but how does one position for it and profit when it happens?

Investment Ideas and Strategies

We should be using Nature's inexhaustible sources of energy—sun, wind and tide. I'd put my money on the sun and solar energy. What a source of power! I hope we don't have to wait until oil and coal run out before we tackle that.

—Thomas Alva Edison

The final component of the next super boom is enabling technology. We won't claim that we can foresee the future and know for certain what the next enabling technology will be—not even Steve Jobs can do that—but we have a couple of ideas.

In the 1970s, Yale believed that the future was in microprocessors, computing, and communication, but he could never have foretold the coming of the Internet. We suspect that the next revolutionary technology could come from several sectors that are primed to have a huge global impact on the everyday lives of billions of people, just as cell phones, computers, and the Internet did in the last two decades of the twentieth century.

Sectors such as energy technology, more specifically alternative energy, robotics, biotechnology, and genomics all have enormous potential to revolutionize the world. And, of course, there's the very likely possibility that something unimaginable will appear in an as-of-yet undefined sector.

Oil spills, climate change, and high prices are making it more apparent that we need better ways to feed our power-hungry gadgets, homes, vehicles, and society. As government initiatives make investments in alternative energy and off-the-grid solutions become more cost-effective, innovation is bound to materialize. Outfitting the planet could generate a boom. Bringing our infrastructure of highways and byways, transportation, communication, and power transmission into the twenty-first century would be a boon for the job market and help fuel a boom.

Biotech is promising because of all the health issues and enormous costs that exist. No other field has the potential to impact the world in the way that medical technology does. Cures as opposed to treatments for diseases such as cancer, AIDS, heart disease, or diabetes would change the lives of countless people around the world, create jobs, and generate commerce.

We expect certain investment disciplines and existing sectors to be especially profitable. The growing population will need to be fed. Traditional energy will also remain in demand and be a source of innovation: Natural gas is cheap and abundant and may see greater consumption and higher prices in the future. Coal is the cheapest source of base-load electric generation in emerging markets. These emerging markets will continue to be hotbeds of growth and development.

The next boom may actually be sparked in the BRIC nations, Brazil, Russia, India, China, as they have the money, the young and ambitious populations, and the inflation necessary to spark invention. The rest of Asia and the Middle East, Latin America, as well as Africa are fountains of growth as well.

In this chapter we have compiled a selection of investment recommendations and portfolio ideas to weather the remainder of the current secular bear market and to capitalize on the next super boom. Markets and economies will struggle over the next several years as inflation, hidden or evident, rises. Keep your eye on the future and get ready for the next 500 percent move.

In addition to the technologies and sectors mentioned in Table 10.1, remember that stocks are the best hedge against inflation. The broad market can be bought with impunity when the Dow is below 10,000. Well-chosen small stocks will outperform large stocks. Consistent dividend payers make money in tough markets and are well positioned to take off in booms. Seasonality works well as markets bounce around in trading ranges and during long booms. When a bear market is officially declared over during the next several years, back up the car and load up on stocks.

We tapped Bill Staton, our resident dividend and large cap value guru, for a few foul weather stocks that would fare well once the boom started. His latest book, *Double Your Money in America's Finest Companies®: The Unbeatable Power of Rising Dividends,* was the first installment in our Almanac Investor book series. From his hand-picked list of hundreds of America's Finest Companies® (AFCs), Bill created The Baker's Dozen Guided Portfolio® as a model portfolio consisting of the shares of 13 different AFCs. Since its inception on June 18, 2000, Bill's model Baker's Dozen Guided Portfolio® has gained 246.0 percent as of December 8, 2010, based on a theoretical initial investment of $1,000 made in each of 13 AFC companies. Table 10.2 contains the current 13 Baker's Dozen stocks. You will do well with these shares now, over the next several years, and for the long haul.

More than 35 positions have been sold and replaced since that date (roughly one-third turnover per year), but there are always only 13 AFC companies in the portfolio. The portfolio is also always 100 percent invested in stocks. Over the same time period the major averages have faltered: DJIA +7.7 percent, S&P 500 –17.3 percent, and NASDAQ –34.6 percent.

TABLE 10.1   Super Boom ETFs

		Exchange-Traded Funds for Coming Super Boom		
Symbol	Name	12/17/2010 Close	Net Assets (Millions $)	Top Five Holdings
Alternative Energy				
FAN	First Trust ISE Global Wind Energy	10.16	51.5	Iberdrola Renovables, EDP Renovaveis SA, Repower Systems AG, China Longyuan Power Group-H, Vestas Wind Systems
LIT	Global X Lithium	21.20	121.5	Soc Quimica y Minera ADR, FMC Corp, Rockwood Holdings, A123 Systems, Avalon Rare Metals
URA	Global X Uranium	19.59	125.1	Cameco Corp, Uranium One, Paladin Resources, Denison Mines Corp, Kalahari Minerals
TAN	Guggenheim Solar	7.30	147.7	First Solar, Trina Solar LTD ADR, Renewable Energy Corp, Meyer Burger Technology, MEMC Electronic Materials
NLR	Market Vectors Nuclear Energy	25.84	255.8	Cameco Corp, Paladin Energy, Denison Mines Corp, EDF SA & EDF FP, Exelon Corp
REMX	Market Vectors Rare Earth/ Strategic Metals	20.68	151.9	Iluka Resources, Lynas Corp, Thompson Creek Metals Co, Neo Material Technologies, Titanium Metals Corp

TABLE 10.1   *(Continued)*

| | | 12/17/2010 | Net Assets | |
Symbol	Name	Close	(Millions $)	Top Five Holdings
PBW	PowerShares Wilderhill Clean Energy	10.23	546.2	Tesla Motors, Polypore International, Cree, International Rectifier, Universal Display

Exchange-Traded Funds for Coming Super Boom

Biotechnology and Genomics

Symbol	Name	Close	Net Assets (Millions $)	Top Five Holdings
IBB	iShares NASDAQ Biotechnology	94.19	1474.3	Amgen, TEVA Pharmaceutical, Celgene, Gilead Sciences, Alexion Pharmaceuticals
PBE	PowerShare Dynamic Biotech & Genome	21.88	199.8	Life Technologies Corp, Amgen, Alexion Pharmaceuticals, Illumina, Biogen Idec
XBI	SPDR S&P Biotech	62.88	526.1	Theravance Inc, Pharmasset, Myriad Gentics, Onyx Pharmaceuticals, Alexion Pharmaceuticals

Population Growth

Symbol	Name	Close	Net Assets (Millions $)	Top Five Holdings
MOO	Market Vectors Agribusiness	51.31	2446.1	Deere & Co, Monsanto, Mosaic Co, Wilmar International, Potash Corp of Saskatchewan
PHO	PowerShares Water Resources	19.33	1211.1	Lindsay, Tetra Tech, Valmont Industries, AECOM Technology, URS

(continued)

TABLE 10.1 *(Continued)*

		12/17/2010	Net Assets	
		Exchange-Traded Funds for Coming Super Boom		
Symbol	Name	Close	(Millions $)	Top Five Holdings
Traditional Energy				
FCG	First Trust ISE-Revere Natural Gas	18.89	436.1	Stone Energy Corp, SM Energy, Newfield Exploration, Hess Corp, EXCO Resources
KOL	Market Vectors Coal	44.43	479.6	Joy Global, Peabody Energy, Consol Energy, China Shenhua Energy, China Coal Energy
XOP	SPDR S&P Oil & Gas Exploration & Production	50.61	812.3	Atlas Energy, SM Energy, Newfield Exploration, Tesoro, Exco Resources
Emerging Markets				
FXI	iShares FTSE China 25	42.59	7931.9	China Mobile, China Construction Bank, Ind & Comm Bank of China, CNOOC, China Life Insurance
EWZ	iShares MSCI Brazil	75.69	11429.9	Petrobras -PR, CIA Vale do Rio Doce PR-A, Itau Unibanco, Petrobras, CIA Vale do Rio Doce—ADR
EEM	iShares MSCI Emerging Markets	46.40	47014.1	Samsung, China Mobile, Petrobras -PR, Vale SA Adr, Gazprom
EZA	iShares MSCI South Africa	72.06	660.2	MTN Group, Sasol, Naspers, Anglogold Ashanti, Standard Bank Group

TABLE 10.1 *(Continued)*

		12/17/2010	Net Assets	
Symbol	Name	Close	(Millions $)	Top Five Holdings
AFK	Market Vectors Africa	34.31	103.4	Tullow Oil, Commercial International Bank Egypt, Orascom Construction Industries, Mobile Telecommunications Co, Nigerian Breweries
BRF	Market Vectors Brazil Small-Cap	57.81	1137.0	Diagnosticos da America SA, CETIP SA, Gafisa SA, Cia Hering, Totvs SA
RSX	Market Vectors Russia	37.13	2405.3	Sberbank of Russian Federation, Gazprom, Rosneft, Lukoil, MMC Norilsk Nickel
PIN	PowerShares India	24.49	542.9	Infosys Technologies, Reliance Industries, Oil & Natural Gas Corp, Tat Consultancy, NTPC Ltd

Exchange-Traded Funds for Coming Super Boom

When I asked Bill if he had some favorite stocks for the long haul, he sent over this selection of "ten stocks for years" (see Table 10.3).

Abbott Labs is a financial icon with a nice pipeline of drugs, even as some come off patent over the next few years.

Should a global food crisis arise or not, **Archer Daniels** is well positioned to profit by feeding the world's hungry.

ExxonMobil has more than two proven barrels of oil behind every share, worth about three times the current stock price. Global consumption trends and the existing transportation fleet ensure that oil will remain an important part of everyone's daily life for at least the next 15 years.

TABLE 10.2 Current Baker's Dozen

Bill Staton's Baker's Dozen

Symbol	Name	December 17, 2010		
		Close	P/E	Yield
AFL	AFLAC	$55.56	12.16	2.2%
MMM	3M Co.	$86.37	15.27	2.4%
CVX	Chevron	$88.49	10.56	3.3%
CTAS	Cintas Corp.	$29.19	20.01	1.7%
DOV	Dover Corp.	$57.36	18.02	1.9%
EPD	Enterprise Prod Ptrs	$39.85	23.93	5.7%
IBM	International Business Machines	$145.00	13.18	1.8%
MCD	McDonald's Corp.	$76.81	16.96	3.2%
NUE	Nucor Corp.	$44.58	69.66	3.4%
PEP	PepsiCo	$65.97	16.63	2.9%
SON	Sonoco Products	$33.98	16.24	3.3%
UTX	United Technologies	$78.80	17.19	2.2%
WMT	Wal-Mart Stores	$54.41	13.49	2.2%

TABLE 10.3 Ten for Ten

Ten Stocks for Ten Years & Beyond

Symbol	Name	December 17, 2010		
		Close	P/E	Yield
ABT	Abbott Labs	$44.58	69.66	3.4%
ADM	Archer Daniels	$70.28	10.86	2.4%
XOM	ExxonMobil	$37.40	12.90	2.5%
GD	General Dynamics	$30.03	10.86	2.0%
ITW	Illinois Tool Works	$48.40	15.95	3.7%
IBM	International Business Machines	$72.17	12.78	2.4%
MDT	Medtronic	$54.53	16.96	1.3%
NUE	Nucor Corp.	$54.41	13.49	2.2%
SYK	Stryker Corp.	$145.00	13.18	1.8%
WMT	Wal-Mart	$51.97	15.97	2.6%

President Eisenhower coined the term *military-industrial complex*. It's alive and well and benefiting **General Dynamics** all the way. Large-scale troop deployments may be winding down, but a presence is likely to remain for the foreseeable future, just as troops still remain on the Korean peninsula and in Europe since the Korean War ended in 1953 and World War II ended in 1945, respectively.

Illinois Tool Works is a cheap capital-goods manufacturer operating globally; highly efficient, excellent returns on capital.

International Business Machines is the highest-priced stock in the price-weighted DJIA and carries the most weight, both up and down.

Recently, IBM made a detailed presentation about how they will get to at least $20 earnings per share (EPS) by 2015. That's about $9 more than most recent 12-month trailing earnings. Historically the P/E multiple, on the low side, has been around 15. That same P/E on $20 EPS would vault the price from the current 145.61 to 300 in slightly more than four years, just a wee bit more than a double.

Of the roughly 11,400 points in the current Dow average, IBM accounts for approximately 9 percent or 1,025. A move to 300 would add more than 2,100 points. Thus IBM alone, if all other 29 stocks remain stagnant, could carry the Dow to 13,500.

As people live longer there's a growing need for implantable pacemakers and defibrillators from **Medtronic**. Also, people around the world are growing more and more overweight, putting great strain on their joints, which benefits **Stryker's** orthopedic devices.

Nucor has tremendous operating leverage when the world leaves the most recent steel depression for good, and it has paid higher annual dividends every year since 1974. Steel is a basic building block of nearly everything from transportation and infrastructure to medical devices and equipment.

Wal-Mart's overseas business is growing around 10 percent a year and is now as large as the entire company was 12 years ago. Meanwhile, the stock price is in about the same place as it was then.

Seasonality and the Best Six Months

If the market does not rally, as it should during bullish seasonal periods, it is a sign that other forces are stronger and that when the seasonal period ends those forces will really have their say.

—Edson Gould

There is not a trading strategy, tactic, or methodology I know of that is perfect, but our Best Six Months Switching has an undeniable track record. The Best Six Months are basically the flipside of the old "Sell in May and go away" adage. Market seasonality is a reflection of cultural behavior.

In the old days farming was the big market driver making August the best month. Now it's one of the worst two. This pairs with summer vacation behavior where traders and investors prefer the golf course, beach, or poolside to the trading floor or computer screen. Institutions' efforts to beef up their numbers helps drive the market higher in the fourth quarter, as does holiday shopping.

The New Year tends to bring an influx of bonus money, a positive new-leaf mentality to forecasts and predictions and the anticipation of strong fourth earnings. Trading volume tends to decline throughout the summer and in September there's back-to-school, back-to-work, and end-of-third-quarter portfolio window dressing that has caused stocks to sell off, making it the worst month of the year on average. Though we may be experiencing some shifts in seasonality, the record still shows the clear existence of seasonal trends in the stock market (see Table 10.4).

The changing seasonal landscape has lengthened the favorable season. We have been making adjustments and

TABLE 10.4 $10,000 by Seasonality

$10,000 Invested in Nasdaq, S&P, and Dow
Best versus Worst Months (Since 1971)

Mos.	Best Mos.	Nasdaq	S&P	Dow	Mos.	Worst Mos.	Nasdaq	S&P	Dow
9	Oct 1–Jun 30	$299,440	$147,250	$150,436	3	Jul 1–Sep 30	–$3,656	–$3,279	–$3,233
8	Nov 1–Jun 30	$311,121	$129,433	$150,264	4	Jul 1–Oct 31	–$4,090	–$2,571	–$3,191
8	Oct 1–May 31	$213,192	$124,646	$152,003	4	Jun 1–Sep 30	–$1,198	–$2,119	–$3,387
6	Nov 1–Apr 30	$136,753	$71,500	$114,305	6	May 1–Oct 31	$2,438	$2,247	–$1,753
4	Nov 1–Feb 28	$71,809	$24,033	$30,152	8	Mar 1–Oct 31	$14,614	$21,518	$17,550
3	Nov 1–Jan 31	$80,170	$31,289	$33,292	9	Feb 1–Oct 31	$14,115	$17,287	$16,751

TABLE 10.5 Six-Month Switching Strategy

	DJIA % Change May 1–Oct 31	Investing $10,000	DJIA % Change Nov 1–Apr 30	Investing $10,000
1972	0.1	$10,010	−3.6	$9,640
1973	3.8	$10,390	−12.5	$8,435
1974	−20.5	$8,260	23.4	$10,409
1975	1.8	$8,409	19.2	$12,408
1976	−3.2	$8,140	−3.9	$11,924
1977	−11.7	$7,188	2.3	$12,198
1978	−5.4	$6,800	7.9	$13,162
1979	−4.6	$6,487	0.2	$13,188
1980	13.1	$7,337	7.9	$14,230
1981	−14.6	$6,266	−0.5	$14,159
1982	16.9	$7,325	23.6	$17,501
1983	−0.1	$7,318	−4.4	$16,731
1984	3.1	$7,545	4.2	$17,434
1985	9.2	$8,239	29.8	$22,629
1986	5.3	$8,676	21.8	$27,562
1987	−12.8	$7,565	1.9	$28,086
1988	5.7	$7,996	12.6	$31,625
1989	9.4	$8,748	0.4	$31,752
1990	−8.1	$8,039	18.2	$37,531
1991	6.3	$8,545	9.4	$41,059
1992	−4.0	$8,203	6.2	$43,605
1993	7.4	$8,810	0.03	$43,618
1994	6.2	$9,356	10.6	$48,242
1995	10.0	$10,292	17.1	$56,491
1996	8.3	$11,146	16.2	$65,643
1997	6.2	$11,837	21.8	$79,953
1998	−5.2	$11,221	25.6	$100,421

TABLE 10.5 *(Continued)*

	DJIA % Change May 1–Oct 31	Investing $10,000	DJIA % Change Nov 1–Apr 30	Investing $10,000
1999	–0.5	$11,165	0.04	$100,461
2000	2.2	$11,411	–2.2	$98,251
2001	–15.5	$9,642	9.6	$107,683
2002	–15.6	$8,138	1.0	$108,760
2003	15.6	$9,408	4.3	$113,437
2004	–1.9	$9,229	1.6	$115,252
2005	2.4	$9,450	8.9	$125,509
2006	6.3	$10,045	8.1	$135,675
2007	6.6	$10,708	–8.0	$124,821
2008	–27.3	$7,785	–12.4	$109,343
2009	18.9	$12,732	13.3	$141,422
2010	1.0	$7,863	—	—
Average/Gain	0.4	($2,137)	7.4	$131,422
# Up/Down	23	16	30	8

using timing to get in earlier and stay in longer. After the first back-to-back decline in the Best Six Months since 1974 in 2007–2009 (see Table 10.5), the historically worst months soared in 2009 following the worst financial crisis the world has seen in a hundred years and the worst bear market since the Depression.

This is precisely what transpired back at the bottom in 1974. The strategy excelled during the sideways market of the late 1970s and early 1980s.

In the Meantime: A Trading Strategy Preboom

In our continuing efforts to improve, we combined two of the most pervasive market phenomena: the Best Six Months and the Four-Year Cycle. We've tossed this concept around over the years but were prompted by a subscriber e-mail from G. S. in Carmel, IN. As a longtime *Almanac* reader and market trend analyst G. S. noted "that the only two real trends that have stood the test of time are the Presidential Election cycle and the Seasonal time period cycle."

We first introduced this strategy to *Almanac Investor* newsletter subscribers in October 2006. Recurring seasonal stock market patterns and the Four-Year Presidential Election/Stock Market Cycle have been integral to our research since the first *Almanac* 44 years ago. Yale Hirsch discovered the Best Six Months in 1986, and it has been a cornerstone of our seasonal investment analysis and strategies ever since. Most of the market's gains have occurred during the Best Six Months, and the market generally hits a low point every four years in the first (postelection) or second (midterm) year and exhibits the greatest gains in the third (pre-election) year.

As the market wrestles with Midterm Year machinations and the summer comes to a close, we hit the sweet spot of the four-year cycle. The best two-quarter span runs from the fourth quarter of the midterm year through the first quarter of the pre-election year, averaging 14.4 percent for the Dow, 15.0 percent for the S&P 500, and an amazing 24.0 percent for Nasdaq. This strategy uses the Moving Average Convergence Divergence (MACD) indicator to time exits and entries.

We've gone back to 1949 to include the full four-year cycle that began after World War II with postelection year 1949. Only four trades every four years are needed to nearly triple the results of the Best Six Months (see Tables 10.6 and 10.7). Buy and sell during the postelection and midterm years and then hold from the midterm MACD seasonal buy signal sometime after October 1 and until the postelection MACD seasonal sell signal sometime after April 1, approximately 2.5 years. Better returns, less effort, lower transaction fees, and fewer taxable events.

TABLE 10.6   Four Trades Every Four Years

Year	Worst Six Months May–October	Best Six Months November–April
Post-Election	Sell	Buy
Midterm	Sell	Buy
Pre-Election	Hold	Hold
Election	Hold	Hold

TABLE 10.7   Best Six Months and Presidential Cycle Strategy

Best Six Months+Timing+4-Year Cycle Strategy						
May 1–Oct 31*	DJIA % Change	Investing $10,000	DJIA % Change Nov 1–Apr 30*	Investing $10,000	DJIA % Year's Change Buy and Hold	Investing $10,000
1949	3.0 %	$10,300	17.5 %	$11,750	12.9 %	$11,290
1950	7.3	$11,052	19.7	$14,065	17.6	$13,277
1951		$11,052		$14,065	14.4	$15,189
1952		$11,052		$14,065	8.4	$16,465
1953	0.2	$11,074	17.1	$16,470	−3.8	$15,839
1954	13.5	$12,569	35.7	$22,350	44.0	$22,808
1955		$12,569		$22,350	20.8	$27,552
1956		$12,569		$22,350	2.3	$28,186
1957	−12.3	$11,023	4.9	$23,445	−12.8	$24,578
1958	17.3	$12,930	27.8	$29,963	34.0	$32,935
1959		$12,930		$29,963	16.4	$38,336
1960		$12,930		$29,963	−9.3	$34,771
1961	2.9	$13,305	−1.5	$29,514	18.7	$41,273
1962	−15.3	$11,269	58.5	$46,780	−10.8	$36,816
1963		$11,269		$46,780	17.0	$43,075
1964		$11,269		$46,780	14.6	$49,364

(continued)

TABLE 10.7 *(Continued)*

May 1– Oct 31*	DJIA % Change	Investing $10,000	DJIA % Change Nov 1– Apr 30*	Investing $10,000	DJIA % Year's Change Buy and Hold	Investing $10,000
1965	2.6	$11,562	−2.5	$45,611	10.9	$54,745
1966	−16.4	$9,666	22.2	$55,737	−18.9	$44,398
1967		$9,666		$55,737	15.2	$51,146
1968		$9,666		$55,737	4.3	$53,345
1969	−11.9	$8,516	−6.7	$52,003	−15.2	$45,237
1970	−1.4	$8,397	21.5	$63,184	4.8	$47,408
1971		$8,397		$63,184	6.1	$50,300
1972		$8,397		$63,184	14.6	$57,644
1973	−11.0	$7,473	0.1	$63,247	−16.6	$48,075
1974	−22.4	$5,799	42.5	$90,127	−27.6	$34,806
1975		$5,799		$90,127	38.3	$48,137
1976		$5,799		$90,127	17.9	$56,754
1977	−11.4	$5,138	0.5	$90,578	−17.3	$46,936
1978	−4.5	$4,907	26.8	$114,853	−3.1	$45,481
1979		$4,907		$114,853	4.2	$47,391
1980		$4,907		$114,853	14.9	$54,452
1981	−14.6	$4,191	0.4	$115,312	−9.2	$49,442
1982	15.5	$4,841	25.9	$145,178	19.6	$59,133
1983		$4,841		$145,178	20.3	$71,137
1984		$4,841		$145,178	−3.7	$68,505
1985	7.0	$5,180	38.1	$200,491	27.7	$87,481
1986	−2.8	$5,035	33.2	$267,054	22.6	$107,252
1987		$5,035		$267,054	2.3	$109,719
1988		$5,035		$267,054	11.8	$122,666
1989	9.8	$5,528	3.3	$275,867	27.0	$155,786
1990	−6.7	$5,158	35.1	$372,696	−4.3	$149,087

TABLE 10.7   (Continued)

May 1–Oct 31*	DJIA % Change	Investing $10,000	DJIA % Change Nov 1–Apr 30*	Investing $10,000	DJIA % Year's Change Buy and Hold	Investing $10,000
1991		$5,158		$372,696	20.3	$179,352
1992		$5,158		$372,696	4.20	$186,885
1993	5.5	$5,442	5.6	$393,455	13.7	$212,488
1994	3.7	$5,643	88.2	$740,482	2.1	$216,950
1995		$5,643		$740,482	33.5	$289,628
1996		$5,643		$740,482	26.0	$364,931
1997	3.6	$5,846	18.5	$877,471	22.6	$447,405
1998	−12.4	$5,121	36.3	$1,195,993	16.1	$519,437
1999		$5,121		$1,195,993	25.2	$650,335
2000		$5,121		$1,195,993	−6.2	$610,014
2001	−17.3	$4,235	15.8	$1,384,960	−7.1	$566,703
2002	−25.2	$3,168	34.2	$1,858,616	−16.8	$471,497
2003		$3,168		$1,858,616	25.3	$590,786
2004		$3,168		$1,858,616	3.1	$609,100
2005	−0.5	$3,152	7.7	$2,001,729	−0.6	$605,445
2006	4.7	$3,300	−31.7	$1,367,181	16.3	$704,133
2007		$3,300		$1,367,181	6.4	$749,198
2008		$3,300		$1,367,181	−33.8	$495,969
2009	23.8	$4,085	10.8	$1,514,738	18.8	$589,211
Average	−1.1 %		9.9 %		8.2 %	
# Up	15		27		43	
# Down	16		4		18	
61-Year Gain (Loss)		($5,915)		$1,504,738		$579,211

*MACD and 2.5-year hold lengthen and shorten six-month periods.

This is still one of the best and simplest investment strategies available for the long term. The financial crisis sent the world spinning and was an unstoppable force. During the long "hold" period, implementing a simple trailing stop of 7–10 percent would avoid most losses and preserve gains.

Our Best Months Switching Strategies, found in the *Stock Trader's Almanac,* are simple and reliable with a proven 60-year track record. Thus far we have failed to find a similar trading strategy that even comes close over the past six decades. And to top it off, the seasonal trends have been *improving* since we first discovered them in 1986.

Backtesting to 1925 or even 1896 does not work because the seasonal trends did not exist prior to 1945. Farming made August the best month from 1900 to 1951. Since 1987 it has been the second worst month of the year for the Dow and S&P. Panic caused by the financial crisis in 2007–2008 caused every asset class aside from U.S. Treasuries to decline substantially. But the bulk of the major decline in equities in the worst months of 2008 was sidestepped using these strategies.

This is not a get-rich-quick scheme and it doesn't carry the risk or involvement of complex active investing. The Best Months Switching Strategy is an improvement over traditional buy-and-hold strategies and will allow you to steadily build wealth over time with half the risk (or less) of the classic approach.

A sampling of tradable funds for the Best and Worst Months appears in Table 10.8. These are just a starting point and only skim the surface of possible trading vehicles currently available. Your specific situation and risk tolerance will dictate a suitable choice. If you are trading in a tax-advantaged account such as a company-sponsored 401(k) or Individual Retirement Account (IRA), your investment options may be limited to what has been selected by your employer or IRA administrator. But if you are a self-directed trader with a brokerage account, then you likely have unlimited choices (and perhaps too many).

TABLE 10.8 Best Funds for Switching Strategy

Tradable Best and Worst Months Switching Strategy Funds

Best Months Exchange Traded Funds (ETF)		Worst Months Exchange Traded Funds (ETF)	
Symbol	Name	Symbol	Name
DIA	SPDR Dow Jones Industrial Average	SHY	iShares 1-3 Year Treasury Bond
SPY	SPDR S&P 500	IEI	iShares 3-7 Year Treasury Bond
QQQQ	PowerShares QQQ	IEF	iShares 7-10 Year Treasury Bond
IWM	iShares Russell 2000	TLT	iShares 20+ Year Treasury Bond
Mutual Funds			
VWNDX	Vanguard Windsor Fund	VFSTX	Vanguard Short-Term Investment-Grade Bond Fund
FMAGX	Fidelity Magellan Fund	FBNDX	Fidelity Investment Grade Bond Fund
AMCPX	American Funds AMCAP Fund	ABNDX	American Funds Bond Fund of America
FKCGX	Franklin Flex Cap Growth Fund	FKUSX	Franklin U.S. Government Securities Fund
SECEX	Rydex Large Cap Core Fund	SIUSX	Rydex U.S. Intermediate Bond Fund

Generally speaking, during the Best Months you want to be invested in equities that offer similar exposure to the companies that constitute Dow, S&P 500, and Nasdaq indexes. These would typically be large-cap growth and value stocks as well as technology concerns. Reviewing the holdings of a particular ETF or mutual fund and comparing them to the index members is an excellent way to correlate.

During the Worst Months, switch into Treasury bonds, money market funds, or a bear/short fund. **Federated Prudent Bear** (BEARX) and **Grizzly Short** (GRZZX) worked quite well during the bear market of 2007–2009. Money market funds will be the safest, but are likely to offer the smallest return, while bear/short funds offer potentially greater returns, but more risk. If the market moves sideways or higher during the Worst Months, a bear/short fund is likely to lose money.

Treasuries offer a combination of decent returns with limited risk. In the *2011 Commodity Trader's Almanac*, a detailed study of 30-year Treasury bonds covers their seasonal tendency to advance during summer months as well as a correlating ETF trade. Additional Worst Month possibilities include precious metals and the companies that mine them. **SPDR Gold Shares** (GLD), **Market Vectors Gold Miners** (GDX), and **ETF Securities Physical Swiss Gold** (SGOL) are a few well-recognized names available from the ETF universe. Gold's seasonal price tendencies are also covered.

Throughout the book, I've made an argument for why a super boom is around the corner. In this chapter, I've outlined some potential opportunities for investing in a super boom as well as a new trading strategy for maximizing returns in good or bad markets. Many traders, investors, and pundits see this as a period of gloom and doom, but for me, it's a period of great excitement. The market is poised to post a 500 percent move in the next 15 years and we can profit from it!

Yale Hirsch's 1977 Stock Picks

WITH COMMENTARY BY JEFFREY HIRSCH

Before I make a quick remark about each one of the following 15 recommendations from Yale's 1977 report, I want to make a point about timing purchases of long-term holdings. In our work with stock market seasonality and historical patterns we have found that they are not only useful for short- or intermediate-term trading tactics, but also for timing long-term purchases. Waiting for market weakness, especially during seasonally weak periods and/or during the generally weaker first two years of a president's term as depicted in the four-year presidential election stock market cycle, has proven to be much more beneficial than simply buying and holding.

With the benefit of hindsight and 35 years of study and analysis, it is apparent that instead of just buying the following 15 stocks at the end of 1976 or beginning of 1977 when the market was pushing up on its all-time highs around Dow 1,000, patiently waiting for better buying opportunities in the worst six months of the postelection and midterm years of 1977–1978 and 1981–1982 would have preserved capital and garnered more bang for the buck. Adding some technical timing tools and fundamental analysis to these seasonal and cyclical patterns is even more beneficial.

1. American Cyanamid 25 7/8
Book Value 24, P/E 9, Yield 5.8%

This company has major positions in fertilizers, toiletries and drugs, all of which have strong growth potential. A generous yield along with fine prospects for the future make the stock a top-notch investment for well-defined total return.

American Cyanamid (AC) produced familiar consumer products such as Pine-Sol, Old Spice, and Centrum. AC merged with American Home Products in 1994 for $95 per share after a colorful history of frequently flirting with environmental laws. A 267 percent 1977–1994 gain.

2. American Standard 26 3/8
Book Value 22, P/E 7, Yield 4.9%

After years of stagnation, earnings began a stage of rapid growth in 1973, matched by large increases in dividend payout. Operations in building products, transportation equipment, mining equipment and pollution controls should benefit strongly by the prosperous economy which we foresee for the years ahead. In particular, a construction boom should benefit not only sales but profit margins in the company's plumbing fixtures and heating and air-conditioning equipment, leading to dramatic earnings improvements.

In 1988 American Standard was taken private in a leveraged buyout for $78—a 207 percent gain. After going public again in 1995, in 2007 American Standard broke up its three divisions. The kitchen and bath division was sold (Bain

Capital Partners), WABCO was spun off, and Trane (HVAC) was retained. The company changed its name to Trane on November 28, 2007. Trane was later purchased by Ingersoll Rand (IR) for approximately $46 in cash and stock (0.23 shares).

3. American Tel & Tel 61
Book Value 57, P/E 11, Yield 6.2%

Ma Bell deserves a place as an anchor in every sound long-term portfolio. Earnings have increased steadily and the dividend has been raised every year since 1960 except 1963 and 1971. The company has a strong position not likely to be impaired despite occasional political sniping. Its record is excellent for high-quality service and constantly improving efficiency. The stock became overpriced in the early 1960s and therefore has lagged behind the market in recent years. It now seems to be engaged in catching up. It is still well below its 1964 high of 75, although its earnings have more than doubled since then.

After nearly a decade of litigation—and stock splits of 3–1, 2–1, and 2–1—AT&T's monopoly was broken up by the federal government in 1982 just as the last super boom was about to explode. Return: 456 percent. But the company was rebuilt, buying cell phone and cable TV providers before spinning all that off and being bought by baby bell SBC Communications in 2005 and returning to the Dow under the original name and ticker symbol, AT&T (T).

In 1983, as the divestiture of the Bell System was getting under way, a poster was rumored to be hung at various company worksites that captures the irony of the storied history of Ma Bell: "There are two giant entities at work in our country, and they both have an amazing influence on our daily lives....one has given us radar, sonar, stereo, teletype, the transistor, hearing aids, artificial larynxes, talking movies, and the telephone. The other has given us the Civil War, the Spanish American War, the First

World War, the Second World War, the Korean War, the Vietnam War, double-digit inflation, double-digit unemployment, the Great Depression, the gasoline crisis, and the Watergate fiasco. Guess which one is now trying to tell the other one how to run its business?"

4. Canadian Pacific 16 3/4
Book Value 31, P/E 7, Yield 5.1%

Here is an investment in the Canadian economy. Canadian Pacific runs major railroads, airlines, trucking, and shipping companies in Canada. It also owns interests in Canadian oil, gas, metal, timber, and other natural resources as well as various retail consumer industries. Earnings have tripled since 1971. The stock, however, has barely moved, perhaps due to fears of leftist tendencies by Canada's government. However, the political climate is becoming more favorable, and the enormous growth potential of Canada makes Canadian Pacific a most exciting long-term investment.

Canadian Pacific (CP) transports all the imported Asian goods in the United States and Canada. There was a 3–1 split in 1985. Return: 1,064 percent.

5. Del Monte Corporation 26 1/8
Book Value 31, P/E 6, Yield 5.8%

Del Monte's main field is canning fruits and vegetables. It also distributes other food products and has some diversified subsidiaries. Its fresh fruit business is highly profitable and has high growth potential, as do its international operations. At its current stock price and yield, this company represents excellent value. For comparisons, its stock is still selling below its 1961 level even though earnings have tripled since then.

Del Monte Corp. (DLM) merged with R.J. Reynolds Industries (later RJR Nabisco) in 1979 in a deal valued at approximately $618 million and what appears to have been about $48.50 a share. We found no record of a split, so that's about an 85 percent gain. Piece by piece, RJR sold off Del Monte with the final piece being sold to private investors in 1989. DLM became publicly traded again in 1999.

6. Gulf States Utilities 14 3/8
Book Value 15, P/E 9, Yield 8.0%

W e wanted at least one utility to serve, like AT&T, as an anchor to provide greater stability and higher yield for our portfolio. Gulf States Utilities serves the fast-growing markets of Louisiana and Texas. The regulatory climate in these states is satisfactory. Like AT&T, the utilities became overpriced in the early 1960s but in the 1970s they moved to the opposite extreme. Thus, despite its fine growth record Gulf States Utilities yields 8%, or twice the average yield of the Dow Industrials. Compare that with the 2.5% yield in 1961 when the market looked at utilities as glamour stocks. Gulf States offers high yield and well-defined growth, and could advance dramatically if Wall Street once again spotlights the utilities.

Financial difficulties in the mid-1980s almost bankrupted Gulf States Utilities (GSU). Shares tumbled below $2. GSU was picked up by Entergy in 1994.

7. Honeywell 41 1/2
Book Value 53, P/E 9, Yield 3.8%

H ere, at a lowly price/earnings ratio of 9, is a stock formerly selling at glamorous levels around 30 times earnings. Yet current earnings are close to the peak previously reached in 1973. Honeywell's main field is building and industrial controls. It is also a major manufacturer of computers. Foreign business accounts for a large share of company earnings. Growth potential is exceptional, and a recovery of the price/

earnings ratio to anything approaching earlier levels would mean a doubling or tripling of the stock price.

Honeywell (HON) split 3–2, 2–1, 2–1 and trades around $50 today. A 637 percent return.

8. IBM 260
Book Value 95, P/E 17, Yield 3.5%

This is the only stock in our portfolio which looks high in terms of book value and P/E ratio. Yet IBM is a truly exceptional stock, and is actually at a historically low level. From 1960 to 1973 its P/E remained in the general range of 30 to 45. The superb growth record of IBM, its top-notch management, its strong financial position and impregnable market entrenchment in a prime growth area of the economy make the stock a must for our portfolio.

IBM (IBM) split 4–1, 2–1, 2–1 and trades around $145 today. A 790 percent return.

9. Kimberly Clark 37 7/8
Book Value 37, P/E 7, Yield 4.7%

The company is a leading maker of pulp and paper consumer products, including such entrenched brands as Kleenex tissues and Kotex feminine hygiene products. In addition to manufacturing paper and various specialty products, it owns 1.4 million acres of U.S. timberland. Earnings, which had become rather stagnant in the late 1960s, took off in the year 1971 and since then have quadrupled, oblivious to the 1975 recession. The excellent consumer franchise of this company, and expected foreign gains, should make it a prime investment vehicle for the years ahead.

Including dividends, it looks as if Kimberly Clark (KMB) has returned 2,196 percent to the present day.

10. Monsanto 78 3/4
Book Value 68, P/E 7, Yield 3.6%

B alancing quality, prospects and attractive price, we consider Monsanto the most suitable selection in the Chemicals area. The company has broad exposure in synthetic fibers, agricultural chemicals, petrochemicals and industrial products. Earnings went nowhere in the1960s, as excess capacity in the chemical industry led to repeated price slashing. However, a more rational policy of limiting plant construction in the 1970s has given the chemical industry a new lease on life as a growth industry. Monsanto should benefit from economic growth in the years ahead and particularly from expected increasing demand for agricultural chemicals. At 7 times earnings the stock is considered an exceptionally good value.

Monsanto (MON) has had a colorful history as one would expect of a manufacturer of DDT and Agent Orange. MON merged with Pharmacia and Upjohn. MON was spun off in 2002 to trade again under its current symbol. The new company is still the subject of lawsuits for its past misdeeds.

11. Safeway 43 3/4
Book Value 37, P/E 9, Yield 5.0%

M any retail food chains have high levels of debt and erratic or stagnant earnings records. Giant Safeway is another sort of animal. Debt burden is relatively minor, and the record is one of healthy growth with only minor setbacks. While earnings have tripled since 1961, the stock is only now 30 percent above 1961 levels. In a difficult, competitive industry, Safeway's management has performed remarkably well over many years, and the stock is considered a good investment for well-defined growth in price and dividends.

Safeway (SWY) was taken private in 1986 for $69 per share to avoid a hostile takeover bid.

12. Sun Co 41 1/8
Book Value 44, P/E 6, Yield 4.9%

At least one major oil company belongs in our portfolio. Sun Company was selected partly for its oil reserves and domestic operations which are immune to foreign expropriation. Earnings have been on a strong though irregular upward course for two decades. The price/earnings ratio of the company is remarkably low, both in relation to other stocks and to past levels for this company. Increasing oil prices and growing scarcity of energy resources should be a source of profit to Sun. This, coupled with a return to more normal P/Es, should result in the stock multiplying in value.

Sun Co (SUN), now known as Sunoco, split 2–1 twice and currently trades around 39, +280. Had you owned Sunoco back in 1988 you would have received a distribution of Sun Exploration and Production Company, which changed its name to Oryx Energy and merged with Kerr-McGee in 1999.

13. USLIFE 14 1/8
Book Value 16, P/E 6, Yield 2.9%

Life insurance seems certain to grow, more or less automatically, with increasing national income. Improved medical care and increasing life spans would further augment earnings of life companies. USLIFE is selling at an amazingly low P/E ratio despite rapid earnings growth over many years. This stock is a striking example of how much stock prices depend on public psychology. In the early 1960s, when life stocks were in vogue, USLIFE sold as high as 47 times earnings, as against today's ratio of 6. Normal expected future growth should make this stock and others in its group attractive enough to recapture their former glamour.

USLife was acquired by American General in 1997 for about $50. The record is not entirely clear, but it looks as though between 1977 and 1997, USLife had two 3-for-2 stock splits, reducing the base price above to about 6.25 for a 700 percent gain. Not bad. Then in 2001 AIG acquired American General.

14. Western Bancorp 25 3/4
Book Value 39, P/E 7, Yield 5.5%

A strong bank corporation should participate fully in general economic growth. We preferred one which operated in the fast-growing western states instead of the relatively stagnant, problem-ridden northeast and mid-western industrial areas. Western Bancorp is considered an excellent investment for well-defined appreciation and good yield.

With a long history that traces itself back to 1928 as the original Transamerica Corporation, Western Bancorp changed its name to First Interstate Bancorp in 1981 and split up in 1996 with the West Coast operation going.

15. Woolworth 22 3/4
Book Value 37, P/E 6, Yield 5.3%

In the retail store field, Woolworth is particularly interesting because of its low price/earnings ratio and high yield. Recovery to normal P/E ratio coupled with projected earnings increases should lead to outstanding appreciation of the stock in a strong economy. Earnings should really take off once the British pound stabilizes and restores profitability to this important foreign division.

Woolworth began to decline in the 1980s with several unsuccessful business moves. In 1991 Wal-Mart replaced it in the Dow Jones Industrial Average. The only thing that remains of the original American five-and-dime founded in 1879 is Foot Locker (FL). A less aggressive diversification and expansion model in the 1980s and 1990s and a concentration on the discount roots might have allowed Woolworth to flourish in the currently resilient big box warehouse and discount or dollar stores market.

In conclusion, Yale's was a great portfolio from 1977 to 1982, but in the subsequent stock boom that began in 1982, this portfolio was too conservative. It was too value and yield oriented. The technology revolution that ensued from 1982 to 2000 was driven by developments of the microprocessor and the explosion in consumer electronics and high technology: PCs, Internet, cell phones, and so on. Yale accurately identified the microprocessor, but the companies selected, outside of IBM and Honeywell, were simply not involved; they did go along for a ride, but they were not the leaders. Technology firms like Hewlett-Packard and Intel would have provided much larger returns, like 5,000+ percent.

Shifting political winds and new government regulations also caught many corporations off guard in the late 1970s and early 1980s. President Richard Nixon's executive order that established the Environmental Protection Agency (EPA) in July 1970 eventually led to difficult times for many manufacturers, and chemical companies were especially hard hit. American Cyanamid, Monsanto, and Sun Co (now Sunoco) suffered under the power wielded by the EPA. For our super boom portfolio in Part IV, we have incorporated lessons such as this learned from our own history.

In the end, Yale's stock picks in this report were much more conservative than his forecast and did not reflect the aggressive and cutting-edge high-tech stocks he would recommend over the next couple of decades in his *Smart Money's* "America's Most Undiscovered Companies" feature and in his *Ground Floor* newsletter that started in 1981. In addition to navigating the broad market's gyrations over the next choppy, volatile six years and bringing countless profitable strategies and stock recommendations to readers, his 500 percent move forecast was a bull's-eye, achieved by the S&P in July 1990 and the Dow in May 1992. Most enlightening in the treatment of this epic report was how little has changed in 35 years.

We are still tracking the moves of the British (now in our annual *Commodity Trader's Almanac*) as he mentions under Woolworth. Many of the same stock market and economic indicators remain effective economic barometers today. History indeed repeats, or at least rhymes. The Fed seems to have noticed. We have, too.

APPENDIX

1977 *Smart Money* Newsletter Reprinted

Smart Money™

JANUARY 1977   SPECIAL REPORT

Invitation To A Super Boom

A SUPER-BOOM rarely comes more than once in a generation. Unfortunately, it seems to follow a severely inflationary era which destroys stock values and leaves investors demoralized and disenchanted. Consequently, when the market begins its phoenix-like rise out of the ashes, the average investor, "scarred" and still remembering the pain of the past, fails to recognize the genuine buying opportunity of his lifetime. This report presents what I believe to be most convincing evidence that a SUPER-BOOM has already begun and is now in progress. Don't be late!

Yale Hirsch,
Editor

Smart Money, Copyright © 1977 by The Hirsch Organization Inc., Six Deer Trail, Old Tappan, New Jersey 07675
Published Monthly. Subscription Rate: $50 a year (includes Special Bulletins plus Annual Stock Trader's Almanac.

STOCKS CATCH UP WITH INFLATION EVENTUALLY
500% MOVES AFTER BOTH WW 1 & WW 2
CAN IT HAPPEN AGAIN? DOW 3420?

A number of acrophobes perspired a bit and donned parachutes when the Dow crossed 1000 recently. If they are uneasy now, what will they do if the market climbs higher? And higher? And higher....?

Perhaps we can relieve some of their anxieties by putting Dow 1000 into perspective, considering the extent of inflation we have experienced in recent years and the fact that the market does catch up with inflation eventually.

There have been three highly-inflationary eras since the Civil War's 74 percent rate of inflation. These periods of high inflation were also war-related—World War 1, World War 2 and Vietnam.

WORLD WAR 1

Prices slightly more than doubled in five years between 1915-1920. The Consumers Price Index (1967=100) climbed from approximately 30 to a dizzying 60. While the nation was suffering from two years of severe deflation and depression with stock market prices being slashed in half, the Dow began to rise out of the ashes. From 63.90 on August 24, 1921, it climbed to an intraday high of 386.10 on September 3, 1929, a spectacular **rise of 504 percent** for the 8-year period. Who could have dreamed it? This era likely gave birth to the adage, "Buy 'em and put 'em away."

Bear in mind that the Dow accomplished its feat despite many unfavorable conditions: the growth of communism and the beginning of fascism in Germany and Italy; monetary horrors such as the German "nightmare" inflation and the inability of our Allies to repay their war debts; the Teapot Dome scandal; Prohibition and gangsterism; et al.

Through it all the Dow rolled on!

After World War 1, deflation brought the CPI down to the 50 level where it remained almost stationary throughout most of the twenties. The early thirties' deflation knocked the CPI down further to the 40 level, and there it stayed for the rest of the decade. Interestingly, the rise in stock prices between the 1932 bottom and the 1937 top was quite respectable too—up 384 percent.

WORLD WAR 2

The onset of the war brought about rising prices as usual. This resulted in a 74 percent rise in the cost of living between 1941-1948. The CPI rose from approximately 42 to 73.

After spending three years in the doldrums, the market began a long 16½ year rise on June 14, 1949 at Dow 160.62 (intraday). By January 18, 1966, when the Dow hit 1000.50 (intraday), investors once again had experienced a giant 500-percent climb following a superinflationary period. To be precise, **the rise measured 523 percent.** It should be noted that a small inflationary rate (averaging 1¾ percent a year) accompanied the market rise, bringing the CPI up to the 95 level.

Once again, we must add that the Dow moved up despite many unsettling events along the way: the Korean War; the French defeat and withdrawal from Vietnam; McCarthyism; revolts in Poland, Hungary, Argentina; the Egyptian seizure of the Suez Canal and war with Israel, France and Britain; the Black Liberation movement; the Cuban missile crisis; the Kennedy assassination; etc.

VIETNAM WAR

The last decade has brought back a crunching inflation, unseen for a generation. War, as usual was primarily responsible. Vietnam helped drive the CPI up from 95 to last year's 166, an increase of 75 percent.

Now, the market is "up at bat" again for the third time in a century following a war-induced, extraordinary inflation. On the two previous occasions, we witnessed smashing moves of over 500 percent. A similar move this time around from the fall 1974 bottom of Dow 570 would bring us—fasten your seat-belts—up to **Dow 3420!**

Before anyone calls us crackpots or superbulls, let's calmly examine some numerical relationships as we attempt to put the 3420 figure into some perspective:

1) We first reached Dow 1000 in early 1966. When we recently, ten years later, hit this level again, it was **not** the same Dow 1000. The Consumers Price Index during the period rose from 95.4 to 166.7—an inflation of 74.7 percent—reducing the purchasing power of the dollar to 57.2 cents. Dow 1000 **now** is really worth only **Dow 572.** To equal 1966's Dow 1000, we should be at the **Dow 1747** level.

2) Earnings on the 30 Dow stocks in 1966 totaled $57.68. This year's earnings should reach $100. We estimate $115 Dow earnings in 1977, twice the earnings of 1966. If earnings are valued in 1977 as they were in 1966, the Dow would have to be 2000.

3) In our May 1975 issue, we explored the case for "Dow 2000 By 1980." Using accepted economic forecasting methods, we projected a Gross National Product of $2.3 trillion (GNP in 1974 was $1.4 trillion). As stock prices and GNP tend to travel along the same general "flight path" (despite occasional divergencies), we were able to graphically demonstrate that the two would cross paths in 1980 at Dow 2000.

4) We also (last year) estimated earnings of $150 for the Dow in 1980—which are not unreasonable. Price earnings ratios over the past 24 years at annual lows and highs have averaged 13-16. On this basis, the Dow could range between 1950-2400. If we take the **Value Line Survey** estimate of $170 earnings for the Dow in 1980, the Average could range between 2210-2720.

5) Assuming an annual 4-5 percent rate of inflation, the CPI should cross 200 sometime in 1980. As the CPI was 95.4 when the Dow first touched the 1000 level in 1966, we would have to see the Dow over 2000 in 1980 just to keep up with inflation. If we take the $170 earnings estimate, which is almost triple the $57.68 earnings of 1966 when the Dow hit 1000, and multiply by the P/E ratio we enjoyed in 1966, we reach Dow 3000.

The last 500 percent move took 16½ years to achieve. If the next one takes the same length of time and began in the fall of 1974, then we have until 1990 to make it **three in a row.**

We are aware that the economy is more mature than in the past and that we can expect revolts, revolutions, environmental problems, monetary crises, scandals, droughts, more inflation, a few recessions and bear markets, not to mention a "plague" or two along the way. However, during the two previous 500 percent moves—or for that matter, the last 5,000 or more years—people always were afraid of something or other in the future. Somehow, we do seem to survive and overcome adversity.

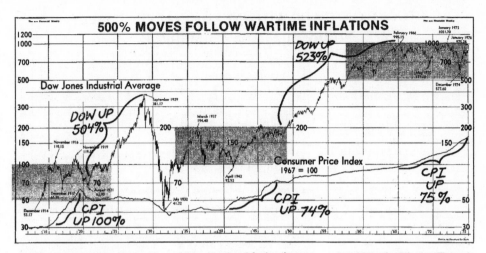

From the chart showing the Dow and the consumer price index plotted together, we first observed the correlation between war, inflation and the subsequent catchup by the market.

We further noticed the rectangular consolidation areas of approximately 18 years in length and having the same percentage range. These give the appearance of "launching pads" for the giant moves.

The inflation/ catchup correlation is clear. World War I inflation (up 100%) followed by the 504% rise in stock prices during the Twenties. Then we see the inflation of World War II (up 74%) and the subsequent long rise of the Dow of 523%. Finally, the Vietnam inflation of 75% (and not over yet) appears and the market begins its next(?) 500% rise from Dow 570 (intraday) in fall 1974 to...Dow 3420?

U.S. ENTERING ONE OF THE MOST PROSPEROUS PERIODS IN ITS HISTORY

Today most of the public and the pundits alike are worried. Some forsee a new surge of wild inflation followed by a crash. Others think the recovery is giving way to stagnation or a new slump. The one thing that hardly anyone expects is a long, healthy period of prosperity without serious recession or inflationary excesses. Therefore the theory of contrary opinion tells us that this is just what to look for.

The very factors that are being viewed with alarm are building the base for such a prosperous era. The slowdown in the recovery is allowing banks and business to **build up liquidity** needed for healthy future growth. Low levels of capital spending and building are creating **pent-up demand** which is certain to stimulate the economy in the future. The widespread **skepticism and uncertainty is itself healthy** —just the opposite of the universal enthusiasm and optimism during a dangerous runaway boom.

But what about unemployment which is high and has increased lately?

Isn't this a sign of trouble? No, it is just the opposite. Actually, **total employment has increased briskly** since the recession bottomed out last year. But the labor force has been growing at a tremendous rate due to a large influx of young people and married women, so business has not yet been able to absorb all the new job seekers.

A huge increase in our labor force is good. It means more production, larger capital investment, more goods and higher living standards. It also means growth in business and hence more earnings. This is particularly true since an increasing labor force allows employers to be more selective and hence favors greater productivity. These simple truths tend to be overlooked these days because of the annoying but temporary unemployment problem which attracts so much attention.

A large increase in total production will also serve to check inflation. Since inflation results from there being more money around than goods to buy, increasing the supply of goods to match

money supply is a very effective way of halting it. When goods are scarce it's easy for suppliers to raise prices. When goods are abundant, competition to sell forces prices down.

Another factor contributing to productivity is technology, particularly the rapid introduction of new microcomputers based on single-chip circuits. These are being introduced into automobiles, appliances and above all into factory control systems, with tremendous improvements in efficiency. The results over the next decade will be a second industrial revolution.

Finally, there is the shift in general psychology away from the extremism and anger of a few years ago toward a more moderate, pragmatic attitude.

It is has been in just such periods in the past that the stock market has made its most prolonged and biggest advances. And as **Business Week** noted in January, at the start of the final quarter of the 20th Century, the last 25 years of a century have been historically periods of great economic activity.

PAGE 3

SUPER-BOOM AHEAD?
HAPPY BIRTHDAY, AMERICA!

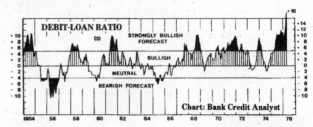

One of the most useful indicators predicting future business conditions is the **Debit/ Loan ratio**, monitored by Bank Credit Analyst of Montreal. This is the ratio of bank debits to business loans at the banks. Bank debits are simply check clearings, a measure of the rate at which money is turning over and hence a measure of business activity.

The logic of this indicator is that if business is expanding much faster than debt is increasing, the situation is healthy. If on the other hand large increases in debt are needed to support slow gains in business activity, you have a weak, dangerous situation. The record shows that this debit/ loan ratio has been excellent in predicting business profits.

During the last thirty years, this indicator has reached peaks as high as +8 to +12, usually in "boom buildup" periods such as 1954, 1961 and 1971. The latest reading, however, has run off the scale at +18. You have to go back to the giant wartime (World War II) business expansion to find anything comparable.

While the debit/ loan ratio has only a fair record as a stock market indicator, it may be telling us something very

important about stocks as of now. With the price/ earnings ratio of the Dow recently under 12 (and many secondary stocks much cheaper), the market should certainly go higher unless the business recovery starts to falter. But the debit/ loan ratio says that, on the contrary, business earnings will go much higher. The conclusion as to the stock market seems obvious. Prices should go to much higher levels despite normal reactions and consolidations from time to time.

The accompanying chart of the Bank Credit Analyst's Debit-Loan Ratio portrays an extremely bullish picture. This ratio is high (and bullish) when business is expanding without a sig-

nificant increase in borrowing and low (and bearish) when business is flat or declining in face of rapid expansion in borrowing. This confirms other data, all of which points toward greater business liquidity. The recession scared businessmen into cleaning up their balance sheets instead of planning for endless growth on borrowed money.

It is precisely such a sound financial base that has been needed to launch a sustained era of high prosperity. In the last decade, as soon as the economy warmed up, it became subject to strains from tight money and excessive debt. This time should be different, and that is what so many perpetual pessimists have not yet recognized.

MORE EVIDENCE OF A BOOM IN THE MAKING

An excessive spurt in business loans usually spells trouble ahead for the economy. It means that businesses are taking on heavy risks. They may be doing this through necessity, to finance slow-moving inventory, or through over-optimism leading to a big expansion in plant capacity. In either case they will be vulnerable to any economic slowdown. The sharp rise in debt in 1973-1974 contributed greatly to the severity of that recession.

On the other hand a sharp reduction in debt places businesses on a sounder footing. With the burden of interest charges and debt repayment behind them, companies are financially healthier and the stage is set for expansion. A look at the chart shows that business has been moving into such a strong position over the last 18 months.

Business bank loans have decreased more than at any time in over twenty years, both in absolute terms and percentagewise.

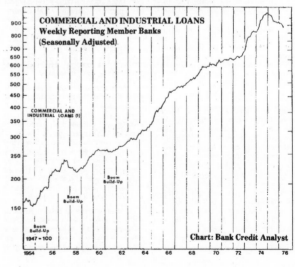

IS MASSIVE RISE IN EARNINGS
BEING OVERLOOKED BY INVESTORS?

Corporate earnings have been soaring at a rate which could soon carry them to 1974 levels. What's more, these earnings are for real—they cannot be attributed to phony inventory writeups. There is every reason to expect them to go much higher since the recovery is still in an early stage.

The stage for a healthy recovery has been set by the 1973-1974 recession which forced businessmen to reduce inventories, drop unprofitable lines, increase efficiency and build up liquidity. This spells good profits now when business is still recovering and could mean unbelievable gains by the time a real boom develops. **YET** skepticism still prevails among many money managers and especially the investing public · **WHY?**

The answer lies in investor psychology, where extremes in optimism and pessimism are not easily overcome even though a market has turned. At market bottoms disenchantment with common stocks is so great and in-

vestment prospects so bleak that only a handful of courageous or contrary thinking investors are able to exploit bargain prices. Likewise, at market tops, the outlook for the stock market and economy is so convincingly positive that again, only a few are able to see beyond the current euphoria when "business couldn't be better" and "get out at the top." The process of developing confidence following bear-market bottoms and tempering blind optimism after market tops is a gradual one. As a result, a correlation of fundamentals (earnings) to stock prices is often irregular.

For example, during the past fifteen years the market has fluctuated widely but has really only "netted out" a gain of 40 percent or 2½ percent annually (dotted line B'-C'). That's a far cry from the previous 13 years (1948-1961) when the average racked up a 375 percent gain (A'-B').

The trend of corporate profits during these two periods, however, were re-

versed with a gain of 280 percent during the 1961-1975 (B-C) and a mere 30 percent gain between 1948-1961 (A-B) when the market was its strongest. Such lack of correlation of stock prices and earnings between the two periods is mainly attributable to psychological factors. Immediately after World War II, corporate earnings soared but the general opinion was that these earnings were just a fluke, that they would collapse as soon as postwar demand was satisfied and a new depression set in. The market advance of 1948-1961 reflected the gradual development of confidence and belief these earnings levels were real and could even grow. Eventually, by 1961, confidence had given way to overoptimism and many stocks sold at unrealistic prices.

It was only natural then, that for some years after 1961 the market failed to keep up with rising earnings. Even though stocks advanced, they were gradually adjusting to more normal price/earnings ratios.

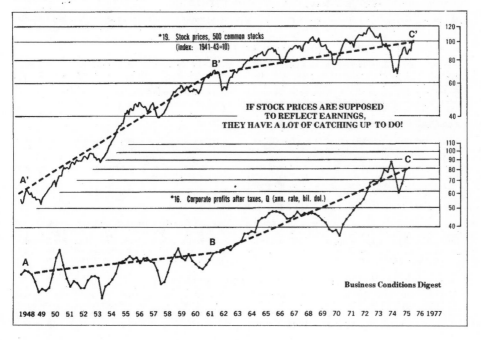

PAGE 5

167

A PORTFOLIO FOR THE SUPERBOOM

How can you benefit most effectively from the superboom which we project for the years ahead? No question but that a good portfolio of stocks should do fabulously well in such a period—but which stocks?

Below we list a core portfolio of fifteen stocks which were carefully chosen to insure full participation in the great bull market which we foresee. They provide a broad diversification, covering areas of the economy which should benefit the most. However, they are not merely a cross-section of the stock market. For example, you'll notice that we have avoided the so-called smokestack stocks such as General Motors, U.S. Steel, etc. Such highly mature industries may show big cyclical flucuations but the thrust of their long-term growth is largely in the past. They are also prime targets for environmentalists, unions and political reformers.

We have omitted companies, however exciting, whose success has been based on narrow spheres of the economy or on specific consumer pref-erences which are subject to change. We don't want an investment based on, say, a bowling boom or some fashion preference which could unexpectedly go down the drain.

We have also avoided companies, however promising, whose stocks sell at high price/earnings multiples. Merck, Burroughs and Eastman are excellent companies, but we don't like paying twenty times earnings. You would be taking the risk that the stock could be clobbered even if the company does quite well, simply because the big institutional investors are disappointed that it didn't do even better. There's no point to making such commitments in a market as rich as the present one is in real **values**.

We have selected the areas of business most likely to benefit from the superboom, and have chosen a stock representing outstanding value in each area. Sometimes this was the leading company in the field. More often it was not, but offered greater value than the leader in terms of its prospects and price appreciation potential. In every instance the stock selected was of high quality, appropriate for holding as a long-term investment.

The average dividend yield of our portfolio is 5.0% and the average price/earnings ratio is 8. Both of these figures are about 20% better than for the Dow industrial average.

This core portfolio is recommended as a long-term commitment for the major part of your investment capital. It would then be held in good markets or bad, regardless of favorable or unfavorable news, for full participation in the big trend. A smaller part of your funds may be reserved for more active management, moving in and out of the market in more volatile stocks, etc. You will feel more secure and more able to trade effectively if you know that you have this solid base of excellent investments providing a substantial, growing field.

By holding such a diversified, high-quality portfolio patiently, we believe you will do far better than the great majority of in-and-out traders who are so busy chasing passing fluctuations that they completely miss the major trend.

1) AMERICAN CYANAMID 25⅐ BOOK VALUE 24 P/E 9 YIELD 5.8

This company has major positions in fertilizers, toiletries and drugs, all of which have strong growth potential. A gen-erous yield along with fine prospects for the future make the stock a top-notch investment for well-defined total return.

2) AMERICAN STANDARD 26⅜ BOOK VALUE 22 P/E 7 YIELD 4.9

After years of stagnation, earnings began a stage of rapid growth in 1973, matched by large increases in dividend payout. Operations in building products, transportation equipment, mining equipment and pollution controls should benefit strongly by the prosperous economy which we foresee for the years ahead. In particular, a construction boom should benefit not only sales but profit margins in the company's plumbing fixtures, heating and air-conditioning equipment, leading to dramatic earnings improvement.

3) AMERICAN TEL & TEL 61 BOOK VALUE 57 P/E 11 YIELD 6.2

Ma Bell deserves a place as an anchor in every sound long-term portfolio. Earnings have increased steadily and the dividend has been raised every year since 1960 except 1963 and 1971. The company has a strong position not likely to be impaired despite occasional political sniping. Its record is excellent for high-quality service and constantly improving efficiency. The stock became overpriced in the early 1960s and therefore has lagged behind the market in recent years. It now seems to be engaged in catching up. It is still well below its 1964 high of 75, although its earnings have more than doubled since then.

4) CANADIAN PACIFIC 16¾ BOOK VALUE 31 P/E 7 YIELD 5.1

Here is an investment in the Canadian economy. Canadian Pacific runs major railroads, airlines, trucking and shipping companies in Canada. It also owns interests in Canadian oil, gas, metal, timber and other natural resources as well as various retail consumer industries. Earnings have tripled since 1971. The stock, however, has barely moved, perhaps due to fears of leftist tendencies by Canada's government. However, the political climate is becoming more favorable, and the enormous growth potential of Canada makes Canadian Pacific a most exciting long-term investment.

5) DEL MONTE CORPORATION 26⅛ BOOK VALUE 31 P/E 6 YIELD 5.8

Del Monte's main field is canning fruits and vegetables. It also distributes other food products and has some diversified subsidiaries. Its fresh fruit business is highly profitable and has high growth potential, as do its international opera-tions. At its current price and yield, this company represents excellent value. For comparison, its stock is still selling below its 1961 level even though earnings have tripled since then.

PAGE 6

6) GULF STATES UTILITIES 14⅜ BOOK VALUE 15 P/E 9 YIELD 8.0

We wanted at least one utility to serve, like AT&T, as an anchor to provide greater stability and higher yield for our portfolio. Gulf States Utilities serves the fast-growing markets of Louisiana and Texas. The regulatory climate in these states is satisfactory. Like AT&T, the utilities became overpriced in the early 1960s but in the 1970s they moved to the opposite extreme. Thus, despite its fine growth record

Gulf States Utilities yields 8%, or twice the average yield of the Dow Industrials. Compare that with the 2.5% yield in 1961 when the market looked at utilities as glamour stocks. Gulf States offers high yield and well-defined growth, and could advance dramatically if Wall Street once again spotlights the utilities.

7) HONEYWELL 41½ BOOK VALUE 53 P/E 9 YIELD 3.8

Here, at a lowly price/earnings ratio of 9, is a stock formerly selling at glamorous levels around 30 times earnings. Honeywell's main field is building and industrial controls. It is also a major manufacturer of

computers. Foreign business accounts for a large share of company's earnings. Growth potential is exceptional, and a recovery of the price/earnings ratio to anything approaching earlier levels would mean a doubling or tripling of the stock price.

8) IBM 260 BOOK VALUE 95 P/E 17 YIELD 3.5

This is the only stock in our portfolio which looks high in terms of book value and P/E ratio. Yet IBM is a truly exceptional stock, and is actually at a historically low level. From 1960 to 1973 its P/E remained in the general range of

30 to 45. The superb growth record of IBM, its top-notch management, its strong financial position and impregnable market entrenchment in prime growth area of the economy make the stock a must for our portfolio.

9) KIMBERLY CLARK 37⅞ BOOK VALUE 37 P/E 7 YIELD 4.7

The company is a leading maker of pulp and paper consumer products, including such entrenched brands as Kleenex tissues and Kotex feminine hygiene products. In addition to manufacturing paper and various specialty products, it owns 1.4 million acres of U.S. timberland. Earnings, which had

become rather stagnant in the late 1960s, took off in the year 1971 and since then have quadrupled, oblivious to the 1975 recession. The excellent consumer franchise of this company, and expected foreign gains, should make it a prime investment vehicle for the years ahead.

10) MONSANTO 78¾ BOOK VALUE 68 P/E 7 YIELD 3.6

Balancing quality, prospects and attractive price, we consider Monsanto the most suitable selection in the important Chemicals area. The company has broad exposure in synthetic fibers, agricultural chemicals, petrochemicals and industrial products. Earnings went nowhere in the 1960s, as excess capacity in the chemical industry led to repeated price slashing. However, a more rational policy of

limiting plant construction in the 1970s has given the chemical industry a new lease on life as a growth industry. Monsanto should benefit from economic growth in the years ahead and particularly from expected increasing demand for agricultural chemicals. At 7 times earnings the stock is considered an exceptionally good value.

11) SAFEWAY 43¾ BOOK VALUE 37 P/E 9 YIELD 5.0

Many retail food chains have high levels of debt and erratic or stagnant earnings records. Giant Safeway is another sort of animal. Debt burden is relatively minor, and the record is one of healthy growth with only minor setbacks. While earnings have tripled since 1961, the stock is only now 30

percent above 1961 levels. In a difficult, competitive industry, Safeway's management has performed remarkably well over many years, and the stock is considered a good investment for well-defined growth in price and dividends.

12) SUN CO. 41⅛ BOOK VALUE 44 P/E 6 YIELD 4.9

At least one major oil company belongs in our portfolio. Sun Company was selected partly for its oil reserves and domestic operations which are immune to foreign expropriation. Earnings have been on a strong though irregular upward course for two decades. The price/earnings ratio of

the company is remarkably low, both in relation to other stocks and to past levels for this company. Increasing oil prices and growing scarcity of energy resources should be a source of profit to Sun. This, coupled with a return to more normal P/Es, should result in the stock multiplying in value.

13) USLIFE 14⅛ BOOK VALUE 16 P/E 6 YIELD 2.9

Life insurance seems certain to grow, more or less automatically, with increasing national income. Improved medical care and increasing life spans would further augment earnings of life companies. USLIFE is selling at an amazingly low P/E ratio despite rapid earnings growth over many years. This stock is a striking example of how much stock prices

depend on public psychology. In the early 1960s, when life stocks were in vogue, USLIFE sold as high as 47 times earnings, as against today's ratio of 6. Normal expected future growth should make this stock and others in its group attractive enough to recapture their former glamour.

CONTINUED ON PAGE 8

A PORTFOLIO FOR THE SUPERBOOM CONTINUED FROM PREVIOUS PAGE

14) WESTERN BANCORP. 25¾ BOOK VALUE 39 P/E 7 YIELD 5.5

A strong bank corporation should participate fully in general economic growth. We preferred one which operated in the fast-growing western states instead of the relatively stagnant, problem-ridden northeast and mid-western industrial areas. Western Bancorp is considered an excellent investment for well-defined appreciation and good yield.

15) WOOLWORTH 22¾ BOOK VALUE 37 P/E 6 YIELD 5.3

In the retail store field, Woolworth is particularly interesting because of its low price/earnings ratio and high yield. Recovery to normal P/E ratio coupled with projected earnings increases should lead to outstanding appreciation of the stock in a strong economy. Earnings should really take off once the British pound stabilizes and restores profitability to this important foreign division.

A PERFECT LONG-TERM INFLATION HEDGE?
WHY THE STOCK MARKET OF COURSE!

Yes! Not once in this century has the market failed to conquer inflation over **any** 25-year period. A $1,000 investment in the Dow Jones industrials for all the 23 periods below **with dividends reinvested annually**, less taxes and all buying commissions, would have resulted in a "Total Dow Return" of $11,563, on average. Meanwhile, $1,000 deposited in a typical savings account and earning the prevailing interest rate, compounded annually less taxes, would have grown to only $1,712, on average.

Adjusting for each period's inflation, reduces the "total Dow return" to $5,648 and the savings account's to $853. Only in three of the 23 periods did a typical saver manage to hold onto his original $1,000 worth of purchasing power. Next time a friend gripes about "the market," send him a copy of this page!

WHAT $1,000 GREW TO DURING 25-YEAR PERIODS

25-Year Periods	Total Dow Return*	Regular Savings Account**	Total Dow Return (Adjusted For Inflation)	Regular Savings Account (Adjusted For Inflation)	$1,000 Actual Cash
1928-1953	$2,472	$1,580	$1,575	$1,006	$637
1929-1954	4,272	1,556	2,687	978	629
1930-1955	7,590	1,536	4,744	960	625
1931-1956	15,696	1,524	8,918	865	568
1932-1957	17,451	1,519	8,513	740	488
1933-1958	13,998	1,522	6,273	682	448
1934-1959	15,593	1,527	7,153	700	459
1935-1960	10,227	1,539	4,713	709	461
1936-1961	9,669	1,559	4,518	728	467
1937-1962	12,500	1,583	5,896	746	472
1938-1963	11,408	1,607	5,209	737	457
1939-1964	13,415	1,634	6,070	739	452
1940-1965	16,472	1,662	7,408	735	442
1941-1966	15,719	1,700	7,145	772	455
1942-1967	16,582	1,739	8,128	852	490
1943-1968	15,047	1,778	7,524	889	500
1944-1969	11,379	1,819	5,471	874	481
1945-1970	9,438	1,867	4,390	868	465
1946-1971	10,842	1,917	5,289	935	488
1947-1972	11,983	1,968	6,408	1,052	535
1948-1973	10,043	2,024	5,429	1,094	541
1949-1974	6,432	2,078	3,092	999	481
1950-1975	7,448	2,129	3,340	954	448
Averages	**$11,563**	**$1,712**	**$5,648**	**$853**	**$500**

* Dividends reinvested annually less 23% income tax and 2% commissions on all purchases. (Capital gains taxes and selling commissions not deducted.)

** Actual N.Y. savings bank accounts with interest compounded annually after 23% income tax.

Key Terms

Bear Market: Ned Davis Research deems that "a bear market requires a 30 percent drop in the Dow Jones Industrial Average after 50 calendar days or 13 percent decline after 145 calendar days. Reversals of 30 percent in the Value Line Geometric Index since 1965 also qualify." Our colleagues over at Standard & Poor's use –20 percent for the equity bear cycles, in addition to other criteria, such as length of time, S&P 500 versus long-term moving averages, and so on.

The Hirsch Organization uses the Ned Davis Research definition of a bear market as it applies to the Dow Jones Industrial Average. The same percentage moves and durations are also used to determine Standard & Poor's 500 and Nasdaq bear markets.

Bull Market: Ned Davis Research classifies a bull market as "a 30 percent rise in the Dow Jones Industrial Average after 50 calendar days or a 13 percent rise after 155 calendar days." Our colleagues over at Standard & Poor's use +20 percent for the equity bull cycles, in addition to other criteria, such as length of time, S&P 500 versus long-term moving averages, and so on.

The Hirsch Organization uses the Ned Davis Research definition of a bull market as it applies to the Dow Jones Industrial Average. The same percentage moves and durations are also used to determine Standard & Poor's 500 and Nasdaq bull markets.

Cyclical: Occurring in cycles as defined by the Oxford English Dictionary.

Cyclical Bear or Bull Market: Refers to cyclical market moves in line with the parameters of the preceding bear and bull market definitions that are mostly less than three years in duration and always less than ten years.

Inflation: A continuing rise in the general price level, usually attributed to an increase in the volume of money and credit relative to available goods and services, as defined by the Merriam-Webster Dictionary.

Secular: Economics (of a fluctuation or trend) occurring or persisting over an indefinitely long period, as defined by the Oxford English Dictionary.

Seasonality: As applied to markets by the Hirsch Organization, seasonality is the predictable cyclical appearance of certain patterns and behaviors. Wall Street moves to a cadence governed by the passage of time controlled by the calendar and clock. Recurring events such as the presidential election cycle, options and futures expirations, tax deadlines, holidays, the opening and closing bell, beginning and end of the trading week, beginning and end of the month, and beginning and end of the year all have a predictable influence on traders and investors, to name just a few influences. The Hirsch Organization has been analyzing data and identifying patterns that result and publishing them for over 44 years in the *Stock Trader's Almanac, Commodity Trader's Almanac, Almanac Investor* e-newsletter, and other forms of media.

Secular Bear Market: Defined by the Hirsch Organization as an extended period of time, lasting at least 10 years, when the market is unable to reach a significant new high. Markets remain range bound and are often impacted by protracted military campaigns. The period 2000 to the present market behavior satisfies our criteria for a secular bear market.

Secular Bull Market: Defined by the Hirsch Organization as an extended period of years when the stock market produces successive new highs and higher lows. From 1982 until 2000 is the most recent occurrence.

Super Boom: A steady rise by a major market index of 500 percent or more over a given period of time, uninterrupted by any significant or long-lasting negative or flat trends.

About the Author

Jeffrey A. Hirsch is president of the Hirsch Organization, editor-in-chief of the *Stock Trader's Almanac®* (Wiley), *Almanac Investor eNewsletter*, www.stocktradersalmanac.com, blog.stocktraderstradersalmanac.com, and editor of the *Commodity Trader's Almanac* (Wiley). He is also a consulting editor on the Almanac Investor series.

He started with the Hirsch Organization in 1990 as a market analyst and historian under the mentorship of his father, Yale Hirsch. He was handed the reins in 2000 and continues to run the operation from his Nyack, New York, offices. Jeffrey regularly appears on major news networks such as CNBC, CNN, Bloomberg, and Fox News, as well as writing numerous financial columns, and he is widely quoted in all of the major newspapers and financial publications.